Rossini

Cover design and art direction by Pearce Marchbank.
Cover photography by Julian Hawkins.
Cover styled by Annie Hanson.

Printed and bound in Austria 1987.

© Nicholas Till 1983.
First published by Midas Books in 1983.
This edition published in 1987 by Omnibus Press, a division of Book Sales Limited.

Order No. OP 44023
ISBN 0.7119.0988.1

Exclusive Distributors:
Book Sales Limited,
8/9 Frith Street,
London W1V 5TZ,
England.
Omnibus Press,
GPO Box 3304,
Sydney,
NSW 2001,
Australia.
To The Music Trade Only:
Music Sales Limited,
8/9 Frith Street,
London W1V 5TZ,
England.
Music Sales Corporation,
24 East 22nd Street,
New York,
N.Y. 10010,
U.S.A.

The Illustrated Lives of the Great Composers.

Rossini

Nicholas Till

Omnibus Press

Other titles in the series

Contents

To my mother

Acknowledgements

I should like to thank John Tyrrell, who very kindly read my manuscript for this book and offered many invaluable suggestions, and Elizabeth Forbes, whose knowledge of the operatic world during Rossini's lifetime is unparalleled, and who went through my manuscript tirelessly weeding out errors and howlers. I should also like to take the opportunity to thank my father and step-mother who have put me up and put up with me during the writing of this book.

A note on the spelling of Rossini's name

The standard spelling of Rossini's first name is Gioacchino, with two 'c's, and this is the spelling I have adhered to. However, Rossini himself spelled his name Gioachino with a single c, and the observant will notice that it is spelt so on his tomb.

1

The pupil of Haydn and Mozart

'Napoleon is dead; but a new conquerer has already revealed himself to the world; and from Moscow to Naples, from London to Vienna, from Paris to Calcutta, his name is on every tongue. The fame of this hero knows no bounds save that of civilisation itself . . .'

This was how in 1824 the great French novelist Henri Beyle, better known as Stendhal, described the thirty-two year old Gioacchino Rossini. Stendhal should always be taken with a pinch of salt, but allowing for his enthusiastically Italophile sentiments, a touch of romantic hyperbole and a bit of pardonable journalese, his statement was not far from the truth. It was only ten years before an opera by Rossini was indeed seen in Calcutta, his *La Cenerentola*.

Rossini was quite possibly the most famous man of his age. His contemporary admirers numbered amongst them George IV of England, King Ferdinand of Naples, and the Tsar Alexander of Russia; the philosophers Hegel and Schopenhauer; the poets Chateaubriand, Heine, and Musset; the novelists Balzac and Dumas *père*; the painter Delacroix. One of the few men who could rival Rossini in fame, Lord Byron, was described by his friend Leigh-Hunt as usually having an air by Rossini on his lips. In Italy, Rossini was described by an English traveller in 1821 as 'the most popular composer of this, or perhaps any other age.' In London Rossini was fêted by the Duke of Wellington, in Paris he was greeted by King Louis XVIII. In Warsaw, Chopin heard nothing but Rossini at the opera, and in St Petersburg Pushkin borrowed an idea for his play *Boris Godunov* from Rossini's *La gazza ladra*. In 1829 Rossini was described as 'The first composer in the world', and Théophile Gautier called him 'The god of modern music.' Rossini was in demand in every capital in Europe, and the descriptions of the popular acclamation he received wherever he went, the brass-bands that played interminable arrangements of his most popular tunes, the banquets attended by the greatest celebrities of the age, soon grow as wearisome to the reader as they must have done to Rossini himself. The adulation that Rossini was shown can only be imagined by referring to the similar treatment received by present-day pop stars, as Byron's description of Rossini's reception in Venice in 1819 makes clear: 'The people followed him about, cut off his hair "for memory"; then he was shouted, and sonneted, and feasted, and immortalised much more than either of the Emperors.'

On Rossini's visit to Vienna in 1822, banquets were given in his

Stendhal. Pseudonym of the French civil servant, diplomat, journalist and novelist Henri Beyle (1783-1843). Stendhal first visted Italy in 1800 with the armies of Napoleon, and returned in 1815. He was a lifelong Italophile and a devotee of Italian opera. His *Rome, Naples and Florence in 1817*, and his journals provide a colourful if often inaccurate account of the period of Rossini's ascendancy in Italy.

honour by Metternich, the architect of post-Napoleonic Europe, who a short while later described Rossini at the Congress of Verona as 'The God of Harmony'. Whilst still in Vienna he was taken to meet the composer whom posterity has chosen to replace him upon Olympus, Beethoven. The deaf, glowering titan praised the young and far more popular Italian for his comic genius, whilst Franz Schubert, far too obscure to meet the visiting celebrity, had in 1817, when Rossini's *Tancredi* first reached Vienna, written two overtures 'In the Italian style', affectionate parodies acknowledging Rossini's widespread popularity, and his 1818 Sixth Symphony has a finale that sounds as if it had been lifted straight from *Il barbiere di Siviglia*. Even Weber's paranoid outbursts against Rossini recognise his fame if not his genius, and Chopin was said to have asked to hear a tune by Rossini as he lay on his deathbed.

Rossini's fame and popularity continued long after he had ceased to compose. One reason for this was his captivating personality, and in particular, his famous wit. In 1829 the Irish novelist Lady Morgan described a discussion held in Paris as to who was the wittiest man in Paris; Stendhal, who was present, named Rossini without hesitation. Few people failed to be won over by Rossini's charm; even Weber, passing through Paris in 1826 on his way to London for his new opera *Oberon*, had to take back the cruel words he had spoken previously about Rossini, and Mendelssohn, who met Rossini in Frankfurt in 1836, and who was rather priggishly suspicious of him, was entranced: 'Intellect, animation and wit sparkle in all his features and in every word, and whoever does not consider him a genius ought to hear him expiating in this way in order to change his opinion.'

In 1832, Alexandre Dumas *père* gave a huge costume ball at which, as far as one can make out, most of Parisian society was present; Rossini, dressed as Figaro, attracted more attention than anyone else, even Lafayette, the last surviving hero of the French Revolution. When Rossini returned to Paris in 1843 after several years absence in Italy, some 2,000 people were said to have queued to visit him over a period of two months. Twelve years later in 1855, he returned to Paris for the last time, and the two most talked about events of the year were the Crimean War and the return of Rossini. By 1855, the Second Empire was in full swing, and there was no shortage of wit and fashion. Rossini was ill and growing old; it was twenty-six years since he had written an opera; Bellini and Donizetti, his successors, were dead, and Verdi, Wagner, Gounod and Offenbach were the opera composers of the new generation. And yet people still flocked to see Rossini, among them Wagner and Verdi, and almost every musician of note who visited Paris between 1855 and 1868. Rossini's Saturday evening soirées were among the most sought after social events in Paris, and when Tito Ricordi, heir to the great publishing house, attended one in 1867, the year before Rossini's death, the crowd was so great that many people were forced to sit on the steps

Rossini's birthplace. A
C19 engraving showing
the house in Pesaro where
Rossini was born.

leading up to the apartment. A year later over 4,000 people
attended the composer's funeral.

Rossini was born on February 29 1792 in Pesaro, a small port
that lies between Rimini and Ancona on the east coast of Italy, and
was then a part of the so-called Papal States. It is a place which
apart from its association with Rossini, who never really
considered it his hometown, can boast little of interest save a fine
altarpiece by Giovanni Bellini in the church of Saint Ubaldo. Both
Rossini's parents were musicians of a sort familiar in most small
towns of the period; neither was properly educated, and his father
Giuseppe's letters show him to have been barely literate,
although he was a member of the august Accademia Filarmonica
in Bologna. Giuseppe came from Lugo, a small commune some
fifteen miles from Ravenna, where he was a kind of odd-job
trumpet and horn player seeking employment wherever he could,
whether as official town-trumpeter in Lugo, a temporary member
of the garrison band at Ferrara, or playing in the orchestra for the
Carnival season at the opera house in Pesaro. In 1790, Giuseppe
secured the more lucrative and permanent post of town-trumpeter
in Pesaro, and at the age of thirty-two took up his new position. In
Pesaro he met Rossini's mother, Anna Guidarini; she was the
daughter of a baker, and when Giuseppe met her, she was earning
her living as a seamstress. They married when she was just twenty,
in September 1791, clearly in some haste, since Gioacchino was
born only five months later.

Rossini's early childhood was spent amidst the turmoil of
revolutionary Europe. In the year of his birth Goethe was moved
by what was taking place in France to write: 'Here and today
begins a new age in the history of the world', and there were few
people in Europe who would have denied the momentousness of
those developments. In 1789 the event which signalled the start of
the French Revolution occurred, the storming of the notorious
Bastille by the Paris mob, and in 1793 the King of France, Louis
XVI, was sent to the guillotine. Ripples of revolutionary fervour
spread from France throughout Europe, and were not long in
reaching Italy. Signs of sympathetic unrest manifested themselves
everywhere, usually fomented by the agents of the Revolutionary
government in Paris. In many cities Jacobin Clubs sprang up, and
in 1794, the year of the Terror in Paris, there was a serious rising
against the Papal government in Bologna, which was soon
suppressed. The previous year, Pesaro itself had shown a
surprising degree of independence when it had objected to a Papal
official in the town, an occurrence which could not have been
imagined five years previously.

In March 1796 the twenty-eight year old Napoleon Bonaparte
was made Commander-in-Chief of the French army in Italy, and
what had until then been no more than a ripple of fervour from
France became a great army which swept through northern Italy
like a wave, and by May had taken the Austrian capital in Italy,
Milan. Napoleon issued a call to the Italians: 'People of Italy, the

Rossini's father Giuseppe
Rossini (1758–1839).

Bonaparte crossing the Alps. By David, 1800. This portrait reflects the heroism of the revolutionary spirit embodied in the young Napoleon.

French army comes to free you of your chains; the French people are the friend of all peoples; come before them with trust; your property, your religion and your customs will be respected.' The Italians, called upon by their rulers to defend their cities against the invader, did so only half-heartedly, and in most places the French troops were welcomed as liberators. This was certainly the case in Pesaro when the French arrived there in February 1797, and Giuseppe Rossini, who was known as 'Vivazza' because of his spirited temperament, was one of the most enthusiastic supporters of the new order. At the ritual 'Tree of Liberty' celebrations which

14

took place wherever the French went, Giuseppe led the orchestra. Unfortunately, the Pesarese were only able to enjoy their new-found freedom for two weeks, for the Pope signed a treaty with the French (The Treaty of Tolentino) which temporarily restored his rule; Giuseppe, who had been too enthusiastic in his support for the French, lost his job. But the local Republicans were not so easily put off; in June and July 1797 the newly created Lombard Republic joined up with Modena, Ferrara and Bologna to form the Cisalpine Republic, under the protection of the French. The new Republic stretched to Rimini, about twenty miles from Pesaro, and in December 1797, the Pesarese Republicans, amongst whom was to be found Giuseppe Rossini, managed to overthrow the Papal government and voted to join the new Cisalpine Republic.

A Tree of Liberty ceremony. The Tree of Liberty, surmounted by a Jacobin cap, was a symbol of the Revolution set up wherever the French went.

15

It seems that the young Gioacchino may have belonged to the band of the Republic's army, either as a mascot or a triangle player; whichever role it was, Rossini was rarely to make such a definite political commitment again in his life.

The fate of Italy was not so easily to be decided. The Austrians, guardians of the Ancien-Régime in Europe, could not allow the new Republic to remain on their doorstep, and in the summer of 1799 they took advantage of Napoleon's absence in Egypt to push the French back across the Alps. The Cisalpine Republic collapsed, and the fortunes of Giuseppe Rossini were once again reversed: he was put in prison. But the political seesaw had not yet come to a halt; by May 1800, Napoleon, now First Consul and effective ruler of France, was back in Italy, and the Austrians were routed at the battle of Marengo. Along with many others, Giuseppe Rossini was set at liberty, and for the next fourteen years Italy was virtually united under various forms of Napoleonic government. Whilst the French rule was scarcely less authoritarian than those which had preceded it, Italy was at least able to enjoy a period of tranquillity and reform, during which the destiny of Napoleonic Europe was fought out elsewhere, on the battlefields of Russia, Austria, Germany and Spain, or on the sea.

Rossini's mother, although musically illiterate, had a fine singing voice, and in 1798 she embarked on a career as an opera singer. It was a wearisome life, trekking from one provincial opera house to the next, no doubt with the usual complement of *Arie di baule* or 'baggage arias'—those pieces which a singer of moderate talent knew by heart and could rely upon to make an effect, and which were inserted into whatever opera was being performed. Anna Rossini's début was made in Bologna, and her greatest moment came when she sang opposite the great contralto Josephina Grassini, as famed for her beauty as for her voice, and one of Napoleon's mistresses. But most of her career was spent in much less exalted company, and she was a great favourite in small towns such as Ieri. It appears that 'Vivazza' accompanied Anna on many of these trips, wherever possible obtaining a position in the opera orchestra; it was on one of these joint visits, to Bologna in 1799, that he was arrested by the Papal authorities for his Republican activities.

The boy Rossini was left in the care of his grandmother while his parents were away, and attended the local school in Pesaro. But he was apparently a difficult child, over-precocious and lively, and was on several occasions sent away to be apprenticed variously to a pork butcher and two different blacksmiths. The pork butcher was in Bologna, and it was during this period that Rossini later said that he learnt to play the harpsichord. Clearly the boy was interested in music, and on one notable occasion in 1802 he was allowed to accompany his parents when his mother appeared in the season at Trieste with Grassini. That same year the family moved back to Giuseppe's home town Lugo, where Gioacchino's abilities were further encouraged. His father taught him to play

Rossini's mother, Anna Guidarini. (1771–1827). In this portrait she is shown dressed for an operatic role.

the horn, and more significantly, Rossini came into contact with two cultivated 'amateurs', brothers and both priests, who introduced him to music-making at a far more sophisticated level than he could ever learn·from his parents. It was here that Rossini first came to know and love the music of Haydn and Mozart, who were still largely unknown or uncared for throughout most of Italy.

The young Rossini had a fine treble voice, and he later said that there had once been a suggestion that he should undergo the necessary surgery to preserve it into manhood, turning him into a *castrato*. In 1804 the twelve-year old boy actually appeared in an opera in Ravenna, replacing an indisposed comic bass, and his voice continued to be fine after he had ceased to be a treble. He was always much in demand later in his life in salons throughout Europe singing and accompanying himself on the piano, and his rendition of Figaro's 'Largo al factotum' from *Il barbiere di Siviglia*, a truly virtuoso piece, was famous, and demanded wherever he went.

In 1804 Anna Rossini was forced to give up singing, and since Gioacchino was now considered old enough to supplement the family income, the Rossinis moved to Bologna, where there were more opportunities for work. Bologna, with its gloomily colonnaded streets has never been an obviously ingratiating city to the visitor, but has always been one of the most prosperous in Italy, and although a part of the Papal States, had long enjoyed a measure of autonomy. Its citizens were famous for their libertarian principles, a trait which appealed especially to Casanova, who wrote: 'There is no town where one can live more freely than in Bologna.'

Bologna. Second city of the Papal State. A view of the arcaded Strada Maggiore. Shelley called Bologna 'a city of colonnades.'

Padre Mattei (1750–1825). Stanislao Mattei was a pupil of the great Padre Martini, whose style he carried into the nineteenth century. He was a notoriously uncommunicative teacher, and when asked by Rossini for explanations of his rules, would reply: 'this is the way it has always been done.'

In 1809 the French annexed the Papal States to the Empire and sent the Pope into exile; Lady Morgan believed that the city particularly prospered under the French, contrasting the 'stirring, bustling tyranny of its military chiefs' with 'that lethargic, benumbing despotism which under Austrian and Papal governments, opposes every development of the physical faculties of the subject'. Stendhal, who admittedly had the engaging habit of finding whichever city he happened to be in preferable to any other, found Bolognese society much less provincial than even that of Milan.

The chief glory of Bologna was its university, and although it was not a great operatic centre like Milan, Venice or Naples, it had long also been an important centre for the academic study of music. The Accademia Filarmonica, founded in 1661, had gained its pre-eminence under the famous Padre Martini, described by the English musicologist Dr Burney in 1771 as 'the deepest theorist of any age or country', and in 1804 Martini's pupil Padre Mattei took over the direction of the newly instituted Liceo, housed in the former convent of San Giacomo. Rossini was admitted to the Liceo, where he studied the cello, piano, and counterpoint under Mattei, in 1806. Although he was technically a pupil until 1810, Rossini's studies at the Liceo were at best sporadic, and when, after four years Padre Mattei, who seems to have despaired of his pupil, told him that he needed to spend a further two years studying plainsong and canon, the already assured young composer felt that he had had enough. In fact Rossini probably benefited more from the fact that Bologna was virtually the only city in Italy that made any attempt to understand or follow the recent developments of music in Germany and Austria. It was the Accademia Filarmonica which had welcomed the fourteen-year old Mozart as a member in 1770, and in 1806 Rossini was admitted as a non-paying, non-voting member, also at the age of fourteen. Another important musical institution in Bolgona was the private Accademia dei Concordi, which was instrumental in promoting the music of Haydn; in 1808 a performance of Haydn's *The Creation* was given by the Accademia dei Concordi, and three years later, Rossini himself conducted a performance of Haydn's *The Seasons* (it is interesting to note that one of Verdi's earliest conducting experiences was with *The Creation*). Rossini's acquaintance with Haydn went beyond this; he apparently embarked on a careful study of many of Haydn's published scores, and made painstaking transcriptions of the string quartets. Although Rossini never completed his official academic training, and was often accused of making elementary mistakes by composers like Spohr, who was appalled by the 'shocking occurrences of consecutive fifths' in Rossini's *L'Italiana in Algeri*, his careful study of Haydn and Mozart suggests that he cannot have been as naïve a composer as is sometimes made out. Rossini himself said that he learned more from Haydn and Mozart than he ever did from Padre Mattei, and in old age described

Mozart as 'the admiration of my youth, the desperation of my mature years, and the consolation of my old age'. He was often accused by his contemporaries in Italy of being too Germanic and complex, especially in his orchestral writing, and one of his many nicknames was 'Il tedeschino', the little German.

Hand in hand with an academic musical training Rossini was gaining a far more valuable practical education. It was largely the result of necessity, for he had to contribute to the family's income. As a singer he was much in demand as a boy soprano in church choirs (women were not allowed to sing in such choirs), but more significant for the future was the money he earned playing the harpsichord in the orchestra for operatic performances in towns like Ravenna, Ferrara, Lugo, and Forlì. It was surely the hard grind of these performances of mediocre operas, performed by mediocre singers, playing with mediocre or worse orchestras that Rossini learned the basics of his future trade; young as he was, he must have been a great deal more musically sophisticated than most of his fellow performers (on one occasion he almost got into serious trouble for presuming to laugh at the deficiencies of a prima donna), and much of the time spent in these orchestras must have been a torment for him. Yet the experience, which would almost certainly have included composing arias for the singers to insert in the operas, coaching the singers, and what passed then for conducting, stood him in good stead, for when the time came to write his first opera, he was able to do so without hesitation or faltering.

All this time Rossini was composing: in 1804 a set of pieces for string quartet; in 1808, *Orfeo*, a cantata for the Liceo whose manuscript shows the hand of Mattei's corrections, and a Sinfonia for orchestra; in 1809 a piece for the prizegiving at the Liceo; as well as church music, and other vocal and instrumental works.

2

Italian opera and European society

Rossini was in many ways an unlikely candidate for the role of the most famous man in Europe; he lacked the self-publicising flamboyance of some of his more overtly romantic contemporaries, and despite the fact that he clearly enjoyed his success, always retained a curiously diffident attitude towards his achievements.

To understand how Rossini's fame came about, one has to understand the role that opera played in early nineteenth-century life, and in particular, Italian opera, for the legacy of the later nineteenth-century musicologists has left us with a somewhat distorted view of the history of western music. It has tended to overemphasize the German symphonic tradition at the expense of the Italian operatic tradition, whereas to most people at the beginning of the nineteenth century, music meant opera, and opera meant Italian opera.

An understanding of opera is essential to an understanding of eighteenth and nineteenth-century Italian society. Some 200 towns in Italy had an opera house, and a town like Piacenza with a population of 25,000 was described by Stendhal as possessing a theatre 'superior in design to any in the whole realm of France'. Smaller towns could only afford one opera season a year, but during this season the opera house and its affairs became the talking point and focus for the whole town. Stendhal has left us a marvellously comic description of just such a season in a small provincial town. First a local notable sets himself up as impresario, and hires a librettist (usually, according to Stendhal, 'a parasitical abbé') a composer, and singers. These then descend on the town, and during the rehearsal period provide a fount of gossip and prurient delight with their scandalous behaviour (opera singers were famous for their lax morals, and to be an opera singer was almost synonymous with being a courtesan in the minds of most people of the period). The first night draws near and the progress of the opera is followed by the townspeople from day to day and then from hour to hour. Finally the great night arrives, the highlight of the year's social calendar. Everyone who can possibly squeeze into the theatre is present, and, as Stendhal observed elsewhere, 'Good honest folk, who order their lives in the strictest economy from one year to the next, will casually squander forty guineas on a box for the first night of a new opera'. For the remainder of the season anyone of any consequence will be found at the opera nightly, and nothing is talked about except the events at the theatre the previous evening.

Large cities like Milan, Naples, or Venice (the three most important operatic centres in Italy, and with Rome, the cities that made Rossini's name famous) which had several theatres could expect to have three seasons of opera: the Carnival season, which lasted from December 26 to Lent; the Easter season; and the Autumn season which lasted until Advent. As the century progressed, performances even continued through Lent, and there need be virtually no time of year during which there was no opera.

Today, La Scala is, with Leonardo's pathetically crumbling fresco of the *Last Supper*, the chief glory of Milan, and probably

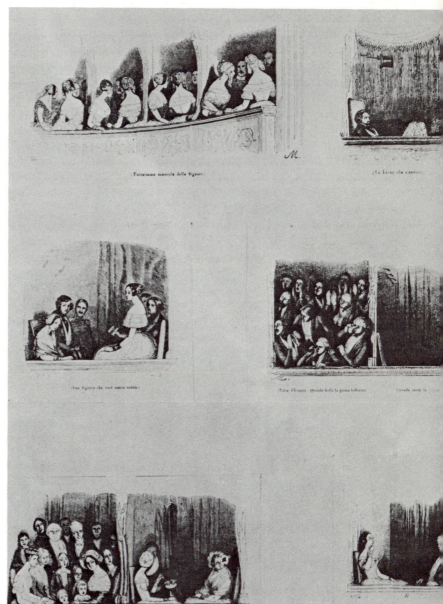

Spectators at the opera. Top row: Ladies' musical enthusiasm. A bored lion. 2nd row: A lady who wants to be seen. Men's box when the prima ballerina is dancing. Bottom row: A crèche. A well (the young couple appear to be conducting a courtship in the depths). Conjugal box. *Il mondo illustrato* 1849.

the most famous opera house in the world. At the beginning of the nineteenth century it was even more important, for it served as the focus of Milan society. Byron, who was in Milan in 1816, wrote that 'All society in Milan is carried on at the opera', and Stendhal described the tiers of privately owned or rented boxes as '200 miniature salons, sufficient to contain all that is of worth and value in Milanese society'. In their boxes people could, as Byron observed, chatter, play cards, 'or anything else', and Samuel Rogers, the English poet who arrived in Milan in 1814, noticed of the boxes that 'sometimes the curtains are drawn, and you may imagine what you please'. Indeed, so busy was the social activity at the opera that very little attention can have been paid to what was going on on the stage. Stendhal wrote that, 'Silence is only observed at premières, or, during subsequent performances, only while one or other of the more memorable passages is being performed. Anyone who wishes to concentrate on watching the opera right through goes and sits in the pit'. Charles Dickens' friend Antonio Gallenga also described an operatic audience at work:

In the pit, in the gallery, in the six tiers of boxes, there are other interests at stake than the catastrophe on stage. Everywhere there is nodding and smiling, and flirting and waving of fans and handkerchiefs; two-thirds at least of the performance are drowned out by the murmur of a general conversation, until occasionally, a burst of applause, or the strokes of the director of the orchestra announce the entrance of a favourite singer, or the prelude to a popular air; when, as if by common accord that confused roar of 6,000 voices is instantly hushed; all laughing, coquetting, and iced-champagne-drinking, are broken short; and all the actors in the minor stages submit themselves for five minutes to behave like a well-mannered and intelligent audience.

The German composer Spohr tells the same story, although with characteristically disapproving tone:

These (the popular arias) were the only items which were accorded any attention. During the imposing overture and a number of highly expressive accompanied recitatives, the noise in the house was such that one could hardly hear the music. There was card playing in most of the boxes, and loud conversation everywhere. For a stranger anxious to listen attentively, nothing more insupportable can be imagined than this infamous din. Attention is hardly to be expected, however, of people who may have heard the same opera thirty or forty times, and whose purpose in attending is exclusively social.

People attended the opera nightly during the season, and in Milan society hostesses knew better than to try to entertain on any day but a Friday, the only night on which there was no performance. Visitors to Milan made straight for La Scala, and could expect to find anyone of note in the city there, as Byron discovered when his physician and travelling companion Dr Polidori found himself on the wrong side of the theatre police, and

La Scala, Milan. Interior view from the stage showing the tiers of private boxes described by Stendhal as 'miniature salons'.

Stendhal and two of the most notable Italian poets of the period, Silvio Pellico and Vincenzo Monti came to the rescue. At La Scala, Stendhal could be sure of finding the liberal editors of the romantic journal *Il conciliatore*, and in his novel *The Charterhouse of Parma* it is to La Scala that Count Mosca comes to meet people with whom he cannot otherwise afford to be seen to be associating.

An added attraction was that the Milan theatres were, until 1815, the only place in the city at which gambling was legally permitted. Samuel Rogers was told that the Rouge-et-Noir tables at La Scala supported the opera house, and Stendhal described how 'In vast halls adjoining the theatres stood faro tables and Rouge-et-Noir and, the Italian being a born gambler, the bank would usually show a more than handsome profit, and so turn over enormous sums to swell the funds of the theatres'. Discussing the closure of the gambling halls by the Austrians in 1815, Stendhal predicted, 'In consequence, both these theatres are doomed, and their great musical traditions will die with them'. Fortunately

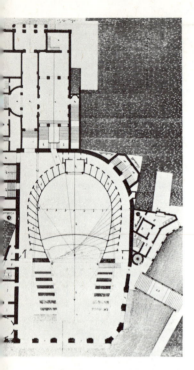

La Fenice, Venice. A groundplan which shows the enormous amount of space devoted to reception rooms. La Fenice was built in 1792 by Antonio Selva.

Stendhal was mistaken, and the Milan theatres continued to flourish without their gaming tables.

When one considers the excruciating boredom suffered by people with too much time and money on their hands, the importance of the opera in social life becomes quite understandable. We have a description by Lady Morgan of a day in the life of a Roman aristocrat of 1822:

The morning is lounged away by the heir to the Gregories and Clements in a dusty greatcoat (the modern Roman toga) rarely changed at any season of the day for a better garb. An early, but not princely, dinner follows; succeeded by the siesta and Corso, a funereal drive in a long narrow street relieved in summer by a splashy course in the Piazza Navona. The prima sera is passed in some noble palace . . . and such conversation ensues as minds without activity or resource may be supposed to supply; a Cicisbeo faithless or betrayed, if at the Carnival, fills up the time till the opera commences.

The story was the same all over Italy, summed up succinctly by Balzac in his novella *Massimilla Doni* when he described daily Italian life: 'In the morning, love; in the evening music; at night, sleep.' He might have observed that at the opera all three could happen together.

The dullness of Italian society was in large measure due to the political situation. None of the Italian states, either under Napoleon or the rulers who followed, enjoyed any more than a nominal form of democracy, and Stendhal and others developed the theory that because the Italians were as a result denied any involvement in the political affairs of their country, they diverted their energies elsewhere, and in particular, towards opera. This was the conclusion that Charles Dickens reached after attending an especially rowdy performance in Genoa when he wrote: 'as there is nothing else of a public nature at which they are allowed to express the least disapprobation, perhaps they are resolved to make the most of this opportunity.' Stendhal believed that the Italians' passion for opera in particular was 'because they have been denied logical thought by Church and state,' and went on to suggest that the authorities actively encouraged the opera, since, as Antonio Gallenga pointed out, 'the effect of music is immediate. It requires no activity on the part of the mind'. One may reject the general truth of this statement, but it has a certain truth insofar as Italian music is concerned. 'Music for the Italians,' wrote Berlioz, 'is a sensual pleasure and nothing more . . . They want a score that, like a plate of macaroni, can be assimilated immediately without their having to think about it or even pay any attention to it'. 'In Italy,' concluded Stendhal, 'all thought is dangerous, and writing the epitome of indiscretion', and there must have been many an Italian who like Alfieri, the greatest Italian tragic playwright, in his youth had no knowledge of literature save that afforded by the opera libretti of Metastasio.

All the same, it would be wrong to see the Italians' love of opera

Italy in 1815. A map showing the divided peninsula after the return of the Austrians in 1814.

as merely a negative reaction to the political situation, as the German poet Heine realised when he recalled a conversation at La Scala between an Englishman and an Italian. ' "You Italians," said the Briton, "seem to be dead to everything but music, this is the only thing still able to excite you." "You wrong us . . . Ah," sighed the Italian, "Italy sits amidst her ruins, dreaming elegiacally, and if sometimes, at the melody of some song, she awakens of a sudden and wildly springs up, this enthusiasm is not

The San Carlo, Naples. The opera house is here being used for a costume ball.

just for the song itself but for the old memories and emotions which the song awakened, which Italy always carried in her heart, and which now pour out in a torrent—and that is the meaning of that mad uproar you heard in La Scala." '

This is an early, and indirect, expression of nationalistic sentiments. Until 1796 Italy was a conglomeration of twelve separate states, of which four were ruled directly or indirectly by the Austrians, four were autonomous Republics, and the remainder ruled by the Pope, the dynasty of the Bourbons in Naples, and the House of Savoy in Turin. Italy was given her first taste of unification under the rule of Napoleon, but became fragmented again in 1815, and large parts of it returned to foreign rulers. One obstacle to any hopes of re-unification was the intense regional chauvinism that the inhabitants of each of these states usually felt for their own state, a chauvinism which manifested itself in the rivalry between the different opera houses from one city to the next. The association between state and opera was especially strong in Turin and Naples, where the chief opera houses, the Reggio Ducale and the San Carlo respectively, served as arenas for state occasions and festivities. One of the first acts of the new Spanish Bourbon régime in Naples was the building of a suitable opera house in 1737, and here the royal house celebrated events such as anniversaries and weddings. In 1815, the year that Rossini arrived in Naples for the first time, the return of King Ferdinand from exile was celebrated in festivities that culminated in a performance at the San Carlo, no doubt as Stendhal wrote of a similar occasion later, in the 'grossest vein of sixteenth-century flattery,' and when two years later the San Carlo had to be rebuilt

26

The bay of Naples. An early C19 print. In the foreground a group of fisherfolk are singing to the accompaniment of a mandolin.

after a fire, Stendhal wrote of the new theatre: 'National pride has sought refuge within its portals . . . It binds the people in fealty and homage to their sovereign far more effectively than any Constitution.' A theatre like the San Carlo, which became an adjunct to the outward trappings of monarchy (and developed an etiquette to match), could even find itself embroiled in political controversy, and Rossini himself got caught up in the struggle between the Monarchists and the Constitutionalists in Naples when the argument moved to the territory of the opera house.

Another obstacle to the growth of Italian supra-nationalism was the lack of a national language. In Germany, a country in a similarly fragmented state, the achievement of a national identity was in large part due to development of a strong national literature; in Italy, due to the lack of a common language, a national literature was slower to come into being. In the absence of such a literature, which might have prepared Italian minds for the concept of unity, and even after the work that is considered the first great work of Italian nineteenth-century national literature was published in 1827, Manzoni's *I promessi sposi*, there can be no doubt that opera served as a substitute, and that the operas of Rossini, Bellini, Donizetti and Verdi were to the nineteenth century Italian what the serialised novels of Dickens, Thackeray, George Eliot and Trollope were to his contemporaries in England.

The Italian people were slower to recognise the possibilities afforded by opera and the opera house for expressions of

27

nationalistic faith than their masters, who kept a wary eye on both. In Milan, both the French and the Austrian occupying powers concocted elaborate rules concerning conduct at La Scala, and in Rome the regulations controlling the theatres verged on the grotesque: there were punishments prescribed for those who hissed or made a noise during a performance, and offenders could be dragged out into the Piazza Navona and given the so called 'cavaletto', or flogged; the German playwright August von Kotzebue tells us that in 1806 'A person presuming to keep a place for another by laying his hat on it, is to be committed to prison'. The priestly authorities may have been stricter than those elsewhere, but there were always police posted in every opera house, as Byron's Dr Polidori discovered to his cost when he inadvertently requested one to remove his hat at a performance at La Scala; and the dying Keats was so depressed by the soldiers at the San Carlo that he decided to move on to Rome, despite his unfit state, not wanting to be buried amongst a people so politically abject. Occasionally the ruling powers had to intervene even more directly, as when in Palermo in 1825 the Viceroy of Sicily himself was forced, due to bad management of the theatre, to settle the choice of repertory and to mediate in an argument over the standard of orchestral playing. A final check on what went on in the opera houses lay in censorship, which could be draconian. In Rome, due to there being three different censors' offices, one each to deal with moral, political and religious issues, forty-one copies of a libretto had to be submitted for inspection, and it was the censorship laws in Naples that finally decided even Donizetti to leave the city, and may have contributed to the depression which led to the suicide there of the great French tenor Adolphe Nourrit.

And yet the opera in Italy was not just a social event in an otherwise dull existence, an alternative to political expression, or the focus for national pride. All visitors noticed the Italians' genuine love and appreciation of music and singing. Lady Blessington, travelling with her husband and Count Alfred d'Orsay in a notorious ménage-à-trois in the 1820s, compared music-making in Italy and England: '*Here* people sing to please; there to surprise; and it must be admitted they generally succeed. *Here*, singers make *you* feel because they feel what they sing . . .,' and in Genoa she observed: 'In the street, voices are heard singing the strains of Rossini with a gusto that is unknown save in the sunny south.' Stendhal wrote: 'I have met with a score of young Neapolitans who could compose a song as unconcernedly as a young man in London writes letters, or young men in Paris pen sets of verses.' Many equated this love of music with the Italians' general uninhibitedness, their innate belief in the principle of '*Dolce far' niente*'. But were this the whole story, it would certainly not explain the Italians' endless demand for new operas. A few composers of the previous generation had become enshrined in popularity, notably Cimarosa and Paisiello, and a work like the former's *Il matrimonio segreto* ('The Secret Marriage') continued to be played well into the nineteenth century; but on the whole, opera audiences demanded new works. This is not surprising, since as we have seen, audiences attended the opera night after night during the season, and a too familiar or a dull work could be deadly, as Lady Morgan unfortunately discovered in Florence, where 'the very tiresome opera of the *Ciabatino medico* was played nightly for two or three months'. Many impresarios when they took on the licence of a theatre for the season had to undertake to mount at least one new work, and the itinerant opera composer setting up camp in one town or city after another was as much a feature of Italian operatic life as was the itinerant singer; such, for the first twelve years of his working life, was Rossini.

Italy was the '*fons et origo*' of operatic activity throughout Europe; everywhere that opera was performed, Italian opera was performed. In the eighteenth century Italian composers were in demand all over Europe, and held posts in innumerable small courts and large households, a composer like Antonio Salieri being held in far higher esteem than his contemporary in Vienna, Mozart. Both Paisiello and Cimarosa worked at the court of Catherine the Great in St. Petersburg, and Cimarosa's operas enjoyed their greatest success in Vienna. When there was not an Italian composer to be had, German and Austrian composers like Handel, Haydn, Gluck or Mozart all wrote Italian operas themselves, and the most influential figure in all eighteenth-century opera was the Italian poet and librettist Metastasio whose librettos were set universally. Writing in 1848, Antonio Gallenga pointed out: 'The Teutonic nations are absurdly unjust to Italian music . . . The opera is their daily food all over the globe.' It had been so for 150 years.

The strongest school of vernacular opera outside Italy was to be found in France, where a clearly individual tradition had grown up. But even here opera had been dominated by Italian composers ever since the 1640s, when Cardinal Mazarin brought Italian opera to Paris. The first important composer of French operas was actually the Florentine Lully, and in the eighteenth century two famous rows had shaken Parisian society over the controversy between French and Italian opera. The Revolution brought a national school of revolutionary opera into being, but one of the most important contributors to the genre was another Florentine, Luigi Cherubini. Napoleon, who had very strong ideas about music and the role that opera should play in his state, once declared: 'The Opéra is the very soul of Paris, as Paris is the soul of France,' and it is not surprising that he brought the opera houses firmly back under state control after a brief period of independence during the Revolution, and then proceeded to guide, and if necessary direct, what went on in them. But Napoleon's own favourite composer was Paisiello, and the two most characteristic Empire operas, *La Vestale* and *Fernand Cortez* were written by another Italian, Gasparo Spontini. Furthermore, there was also in Paris a theatre dedicated to the presentation of solely Italian opera, the Théâtre-Italien. During the period of Rossini's ascendancy in Europe the Théâtre-Italien was undoubtedly far more lively than the French Opéra, and the diaries of an assiduous opera-goer like the painter Eugène Delacroix record that, as most people in Paris, he frequented the Italian opera almost exclusively. The continued vitality of the Théâtre-Italien, despite ups and downs, was due to regular injections of Italian blood, of which the arrival in Paris of Rossini in 1824 was by far the most important. From then on what had hitherto been merely injections of life-blood from Italy became a virtual drain, and by 1831 Mendelssohn was reporting from Italy that all the great singers had left the country to sing in Paris. The singers were followed by the composers, Bellini (who like Rossini died in Paris) in 1834, and Donizetti in 1835. Paradoxically, the rise of French opera after 1830 coincided with the greatest period of the Italian opera in Paris.

The story of domination of operatic life by the Italians is the same all over Europe; Italian opera was truly an international art form. In England any hopes for an English school of opera had died with Henry Purcell in 1695, and apart from the popular ballad operas originally devised by John Gay, and a solitary example of a serious opera, Arne's *Artaxerxes* (based on an Italian libretto by Metastasio), the English relied upon foreign, and especially Italian imports. There was no real competition for the Italian opera at the King's Theatre on the Haymarket, and certainly no rival to Rossini, for 'so entirely did Rossini engross the stage that the operas of no other masters were ever to be heard, with the exception of those of Mozart'. In Austria and Germany, despite the efforts of composers like Weber to institute a national opera, the Italians retained their hold undaunted. In Dresden Weber waged a long feud with the resident Italian composer Morlacchi over the relative status of the German against the Italian opera company, and in Vienna it was the visit of the San Carlo company with Rossini in 1822 which provided the most talked about operatic event of the decade. It was undoubtedly the popularity of Italian opera in Vienna that frustrated the operatic ambitions of Schubert and Beethoven. And so in Prague, and east to Budapest, Warsaw and St. Petersburg, and west to the Americas, where the inhabitants of the new world proved that they were as civilised as anyone by building opera houses and mounting Italian operas, Rossini conquered. In 1829 his reputation was so great that his last opera *Guillaume Tell* had been performed in Brussels, Frankfurt, Budapest, London, Graz, Vienna, Berlin, Brünn and Prague before the year of its opening in Paris was out. By that year Rossini's operas had been performed as far afield as New York, Mexico, Buenos Aires, Rio de Janeiro, Havanna, Philadelphia, Odessa, and Algiers. Another fifteen years, and *La Cenerentola* had reached Australia; Rossini had conquered every inhabited continent on the earth.

3

Venetian apprenticeship

Rossini's first two opera commissions arose, not surprisingly, out of his contact with some of the itinerant performers with whom he worked. The first of these, the Mombelli family, was typical of the picturesque and picaresque figures who populated Italian operatic life at this period. The father, Domenico, had in his day been a fine tenor, and a rival to the elder Davide at the San Carlo. By the time Rossini met him Domenico was fifty-four years old and earned his living as a composer. His wife Vincenzina was the sister of the great Italian choreographer Viganò, whom Rossini was later to come across in Milan. They had two daughters; Ester, the elder, became a contralto with a fine florid technique and a soprano extension at the top end of the voice; sometime later Lady Morgan described her as, 'a charming actress, and exquisite singer,' and went on to explain that 'her most ladylike manners and perfect respectability made her the most popular professional singer in the salons of Rome,' (singers at this time did not have a reputation for respectability). The younger daughter, Mariana, was also a singer, and specialised in travesty roles. The thirteen-year-old Rossini's introduction to the Mombellis in 1805 came about, as he subsequently described, through his remarkable powers of musical memory. He had been asked by a 'lady friend' (Rossini was always eager to relate the amorous escapades of his youth, although on this occasion he must have forgotten how tender his years really were at the time) to secure some music from an opera by Domenico Mombelli currently being performed in Bologna, and on being refused by Mombelli set about getting it down on paper with characteristic determination by attending a performance and then writing it out from memory when he got home. Mombelli was so impressed that he asked the boy to set an operatic text by his wife, which was accordingly sent to the youthful aspirant number by number over a period of time, although it appears to have been completed by 1808. Even so, at this time Ester was still only fourteen and the first performance of *Demetrio e Polibio* had to wait until 1812, when Ester and her sister made their débuts in Rome in the opera.

The second family with whom Rossini came into fruitful contact was the Morandis; of less note than the Mombellis, they were of greater significance to his future career. Giovanni was a composer and chorus master, and his wife Rosa a singer, and, like Rossini's own parents, they travelled around Italy together gaining employment wherever they could. In August 1810, on their way to perform in Venice, they stopped in Bologna and met

Ester Mombelli (b1794). Performed at first with her sister Anna before becoming a well known singer in her own right.

the eighteen-year old Rossini; clearly impressed by his abilities, they seemed to think that there might be something for him in Venice.

Venice in 1810 was a sad city, retaining but a shadow of its former glory. The proud Republic had gone into terminal decline long before the arrival of Napoleon in 1797, and it crumbled at his touch. Napoleon had warned: 'I will stand no more Senates, no more Inquisitions; I will be an Attila for the Venetian state,' and he was true to his word. The Doge was forced to resign, and the oligarchic government which had ruled for so many centuries to disband. The French had looted the city, and taken even the four bronze horses of San Marco which had been in Venice for 790 years, which prompted Samuel Rogers to remark: 'How inhuman to rob them of the only four horses they had,' and then handed the city over to the Austrians, who neglected it sadly until in 1807 the French returned.

The French taking the horses of San Marco in 1798. The horses, a symbol of Venice's glory for almost 800 years, were eventually returned.

The gloomy, crumbling, smelly city held little attraction for the visitor, and it was not until later in the century that its charm and beauty were rediscovered. Byron, who lived in Venice for several years, seems to have found its gloomy atmosphere in accord with his own temperament, but when Shelley came to visit him there in 1818, he wrote:

I do not imagine that it was ever so degraded since the French and especially the Austrian yoke. The Austrians take 60% in taxes, and impose free quarters on the inhabitants. A horde of German soldiers, as vicious and more disgusting than the Venetians themselves insult these miserable people. I had no conception of the excess to which avarice, cowardice, superstition, ignorance, passionless lust, and all the inexpressible brutalities which degrade human nature, could be carried, until I had passed a few days in Venice.

Nonetheless, to Italians in particular, Venice still retained something of the glittering, pleasure-loving reputation that had kept it vicariously alive through the eighteenth century, and is portrayed in the popular imagination by the paintings of Canaletto and Longhi, or in the life of Casanova. More than anywhere else the theatre was an integral part of Venetian life. Eighteenth-century Venice was the home of the playwrights Goldoni and Gozzi, and in 1800 there were eight theatres which performed plays and operas. Venice was the spiritual home of Italian opera; it was in Venice that the first public opera house had been built, and it was Venice which had instituted the idea of a Carnival season of opera. During the Carnival in Rossini's time, theatres were open all day long, with non-stop theatrical performances. The Venetians were famous for their enthusiastic love of theatre and opera and by tradition gondoliers were allowed free admission to the opera.

Domenico Cimarosa (1749–1801). His *Il matrimonio segreto* was so well received by the Emperor Leopold II at its première in Vienna in 1792 that it was repeated, complete, the same night. Cimarosa's comic operas are the greatest stylistic influence upon Rossini.

Of the theatres which presented opera, the most famous were the still flourishing La Fenice (The Phoenix, risen from the flames after one of the periodic fires that few theatres of that age escaped), opened in 1792; the Teatro San Benedetto, the home of comic opera and much frequented a little time later by Byron; and the Teatro San Moisè, built in 1640, which was the home of the popular one-act comic operas called '*farsè*'. It was in a season of *farsè* at the San Moisè that the Morandis were due to perform in 1810. The impresario was the Marchese Cavalli, a figure straight from the pages of Stendhal, a roué aristocrat who enjoyed dabbling in theatricals, and who especially enjoyed what was the virtual 'droit du Seigneur' of any impresario, the right to claim the *prima donna* as his mistress, a right first recorded as long ago as 1720 by Benedetto Marcello in a satirical attack upon operatic life. It was one of these ladies, the soprano Adelaide Carpano, with whom Rossini had crossed swords on one of his stints in the orchestra; she had complained to her lover Cavalli who, not taking the matter too seriously, allowed Rossini to exonerate himself.

33

Giovanni Paisiello (1740–1816). With Cimarosa, the most popular and influential comic opera composer of the late eighteenth century.

Cavalli had a season of five *farsè* planned for the San Moisè, of which four were to be newly written. The composer of one of these had failed to fulfil his contract, and the Morandis suggested that Rossini should be called for. Cavalli may have remembered the boy from a few years earlier, and Rossini hastened across the Po valley to Venice, where he was thrown the libretto for *La cambiale di matrimonio* ('The Bill-of-Exchange of Marriage'), which he set to work on with all speed. During rehearsals Rossini had some trouble with the singers, who found the music too thickly orchestrated, an early indication of a criticism that he was to meet many times later in his career; but with the help of Morandi, the problem was set right, and the opera opened on November 3, 1810.

It would be foolish to go into too lengthy a discussion of *La cambiale*, for it is a fairly slight piece. But what is immediately of note even on a first hearing is that the music is unmistakably Rossini; at the age of eighteen, Rossini had found his voice. In 1810, although opera in Italy was as active as ever, there were very few notable composers at work. The most successful of the late eighteenth-century composers, Domenico Cimarosa, whose *Il matrimonio segreto* was long held up as the supreme model to which all comic operas should aspire, and which well into the 1820s was one of the few operas which could rival those of Rossini in popularity, had died in Venice in 1801, an exile from Naples. His main rival, Giovanni Paisiello, although alive until 1816, gave up composing operas in 1803. It was these two, and their numerous imitators, whom one might have expected to influence Rossini most, for of the still active Italian composers in 1810, Cherubini and Spontini were in Paris writing operas which conformed to the French taste, Paer was working for the Théâtre-Italien in Paris, and the only important composer working in Italy was the German born Johann-Simon Mayr, who was more noted for his sophisticated orchestral writing than for his musical individuality, although his orchestral writing may have influenced Rossini. But *La cambiale* shows Rossini to have been in almost full control of his own style; the music in places lacks dramatic pace and variety, but it is quite without the over-sweet sentimentality that can mark Paisiello's comic operas, and although closest to Cimarosa in style, already has more zest and spirit than anything Cimarosa might have written.

4

First triumphs. Milan, *Tancredi, L'Italiana*

Rossini returned to Bologna for a renewed stint playing in the orchestra of the Teatro del Corso, for operas by Mayr and Domenico Puccini, the grandfather of the more famous Giacomo Puccini. Probably because of his recent experience in Venice, Rossini was also given a commission to write a comic opera, and the result was a two-act piece called *L'equivoco stravagante* ('The Strange Misunderstanding'), which was performed on October 26, 1811. Unfortunately the police considered the plot too risqué (the strange misunderstanding in question concerns whether or not a woman is really a castrato in disguise), and after being allowed to run for the statutory three performances, it was taken off. A contemporary journalist condoned the suppression, stating that the opera contained 'expressions that, when sung, produce an impression not to be tolerated, though they might be tolerated in reading.' Clearly he understood the far greater emotive power of the sung over the written word in Italy.

In December 1811 Rossini returned to Venice to write another *farsa* for the San Moisè, *L'inganno felice* ('The Happy Deception'). The opera opened on January 8, 1812, and its success was hailed with customary Venetian flamboyance, which included the letting loose of pheasants, canaries and doves from the loges of the theatre. The performers included two singers with whom Rossini was to be associated later in his career—Teresa Belloc-Giorgi, whom Stendhal admired greatly when she later created the role of Ninetta in Rossini's *La gazza ladra*, and Filippo Galli, who had started his career as a tenor, made his début as a bass in *La cambiale*, and went on to become one of the greatest basses in Europe, and the creator of many Rossini roles.

In March Rossini was to be found in Ferrara, a city that lies between Venice and Bologna, and which he knew from his orchestral playing days. To get round the Church's interdiction against theatrical performances during Lent, operas were set to biblical subjects and called oratorios, which had the added advantage of providing a whole new source of stories for the hard-pressed librettist, who otherwise had to sort through an all too well-thumbed stock. In this Lent season at Ferrara, Rossini set a libretto entitled *Ciro in Babilonia* ('Cyrus in Babylon'). The cast included one of the most famous singers of the period, Maria Marcolini, the mistress of Napoleon's brother Lucien Bonaparte; but the most famous number in the opera is an '*aria del sorbetto*', written for a rather less talented singer. An 'aria del sorbetto' was an aria sung by a *seconda donna* or *secondo uomo* (as opposed to a

Ciro in Babilonia. A
design by Sanquirico for
a production of the opera
in Milan in 1818.

prima donna or *primo uomo*) during which the audience, knowing
that it was not going to miss anything spectacular, felt it safe to go
and buy the sorbets which were such popular refreshments in
Italy. The *seconda donna* for the performance of *Ciro* was not only
very ugly, but had a voice in which, after careful testing, Rossini
could only find one note that sounded passable; with great
resourcefulness he therefore wrote an aria that consists in the vocal
part of only one repeated note, the middle B flat which Rossini had
decided was acceptable. We should not be surprised by this
curious aria, for it is simply the logical extension of the practice
whereby all composers suited their vocal writing to the performers
at hand. Pacini, later to be associated with Rossini on the
composition of an opera, described how the composer should

always try to serve his singers as a tailor serves his clients, 'concealing the natural defects of the figure and emphasising its good points.' Of course, it could work the other way; Stendhal tells a story about how Rossini, annoyed with Galli for some reason, wrote an entire recitative that centred upon the weakest part of Galli's voice, cruelly exposing it.

Immediately after the opening of *Ciro* Rossini must have hurried back to Venice, for less than a month later, on May 9, another one-act *farsa* called *La scala di seta* ('The Silken Ladder') opened at the San Moisè. We do not know how it was received, but its brilliant overture is still played today in the concert hall.

On May 18, nine days after the opening of *La scala di seta*, the Mombellis finally mounted *Demetrio e Polibio* in Rome; it is virtually impossible that Rossini could have got to Rome for the première of *Demetrio*, which therefore became one of the few operas which he himself was not responsible for bringing to the stage. In June, after the final performance of *La scala*, Rossini returned to his family in Bologna, where his success in Venice soon caught up with him, for through the offices of Marcolini and Galli he received a commission for an opera to be performed at La Scala, Milan in September, for which he was given a libretto by a house librettist at La Scala, Luigi Romanelli, called *La pietra del paragone*, ('The Touchstone').

Eugène de Beauharnais. Viceroy of Italy and Napoleon's step-son. Eugène, a member of Napoleon's extended family which ruled all over Europe, was much loved in Milan.

The Milan in which Rossini arrived in 1812 was a rapidly expanding city with a population that had grown from 120,000 to 140,000 in the ten years following Napoleon's first entry into the city, in 1796. It was the capital of the kingdom of Lombardy which Napoleon had created in 1805 with himself as King, a year after having crowned himself Emperor of France. As was his custom wherever possible he appointed one of his relatives to rule in his place, in this case his step-son Eugène de Beauharnais, who was created Viceroy. Eugène, closely supervised by Napoleon from Paris, instituted a comprehensive series of reforms, which included a large scale building programme of houses, canals and roads, the completion of the still unfinished Gothic cathedral, the laying out of public gardens, sanitation improvements, and the establishing of French-style lycées. Eugène himself provided the focus for a far more glittering society than Milan, hitherto rather restricted by being a provincial Austrian outpost, had ever known. Stendhal found Milan the most invigorating city in Italy, a fact which he attributed without question to the French influence, and wrote in 1816: 'I should never leave Milan . . . if I were to follow my inclinations, I should spend all my leave in Milan. I have never met people I find so easy to take to my heart . . . it is the *ensemble* of its ways, the naturalness of its manners, its good nature, its great art of being happy.' Even from Stendhal that is high praise for a city.

As we have already seen (Chapter 2), La Scala was the centre of all social activity in Milan. The theatre had been built in 1778 to replace, like La Fenice in Venice, a theatre burned down a few years previously, and like La Fenice, it was owned by its shareholders, who either used the hundred or so private boxes themselves, or rented them out. One of the most complete contemporary descriptions of La Scala is that by Samuel Rogers, who visited it in 1814. He was greatly impressed:

The house vast and simple in design, the boxes circling in parallel lines hung with blue or yellow silk alternately from the floor to the roof; and all receiving light only from the stage; except in a few instances; where the figures being illuminated from within, the glimmering and partial lights had a very visionary and magical effect.

On another occasion he noted not only 'the magnificent salle', but also the 'deep and splendid stage'. It was the stage which was the real glory of La Scala, for the splendour of its scenic designs far surpassed anything which was to be seen elsewhere in Italy and most of Europe. This was due to the presence in Milan of the great stage designer Alessandro Sanquirico, who was born in 1777, and was active at La Scala until 1832. Sanquirico's monumental architectural designs, several of which were for new operas by Rossini, introduced new standards into the visual aspect of opera. Stendhal, arriving from Paris in 1816, was bowled over on his first visit to La Scala:

La Scala, Milan, c1812. Engraving by Stucchi showing the theatre as it must have appeared to Rossini in 1812, the year of his arrival in the city.

The whole stage of La Scala is afire with wealth and magnificence; the crowd of singers and actors rarely numbers less than a hundred at any given moment; and one and all are costumed with a splendour which, in France, would be reserved most severely for the star performers.

On another occasion he recorded no less than eleven changes of scenery during one performance. As he was later to write about a performance of Rossini's *Bianca e Faliero* in 1819:

Nothing disposes one better to be moved by the music than the slight shiver of pleasure that one feels at La Scala as the curtain rises, at the first sight of a superb piece of scenery.

Sanquirico was essentially a neo-classicist, although he adapted his vision to the requirements of romantic opera; Stendhal, referring to the French neo-classical painter, called Sanquirico's designs 'David transported into the medium of decor'. Rejecting the fantasy associated with eighteenth-century theatre design, Sanquirico's impact was based on monumental architectural decors, often with a great deal of historical detail and authenticity. Sanquirico also insisted that the auditorium be dimmed during the performance (an innovation often attributed to Wagner), thus emphasising the importance of the stage picture, and he was responsible for experimenting with gas lighting in the theatre, one of the most important steps toward the theatrical illusionism which dominated the later nineteenth-century stage. In 1830 Sanquirico designed the present interior of La Scala.

Sanquirico's design for a revival of Mozart's *La clemenza di Tito*, showing his use of massive architectural scenery.

The second important contemporary of Rossini at La Scala was the choreographer Viganò, whose sister was married to Domenico Mombelli. The ballet was an integral part of an evening at the opera, for it was customary to have a serious ballet following the first act of an opera, and a comic ballet following the second; occasionally there was also a ballet after the opera was over. When Spohr attended La Scala in 1816 he recorded: 'After the first act of the opera came a large, serious ballet, distinguished by the skill of a number of dancers and by the splendour of the costumes and decorations. It lasted nearly an hour, so that the first act of the opera had been fairly forgotten.'

Viganò was recognised as the greatest choreographer of the age, and his ballets were taken as seriously by connoisseurs as the opera. In 1801 he had collaborated with Beethoven in Vienna on the ballet *Prometheus*, but in Italy his most famous creations were his dramatic ballets, in particular his version of *Othello*. Shelley, who attended a performance at La Scala in April 1818 was clearly more impressed by the ballet than by the opera, and wrote in a letter home:

Viganò's ballet *Dedalo* (1817) at La Scala. Designed by Sanquirico.

The opera is very good, and the house larger, or at least as large as that of London. They have Mad Camporese here as the prima-donna—a cold and unfeeling singer and a bad actress. Their ballets, which are a kind of pantomime dance illustrative of some story, are much superior to anything of their kind in England . . . in *Othello* the story is so well told in action as to leave upon the mind an impression as of a real tragedy.

Stendhal, who was inclined to get carried away in his enthusiasm for Viganò, believed that Viganò was one of the few people who could compare with Rossini, writing: 'Shakespeare's most beautiful tragedy does not produce upon me one half the effect of a ballet by Viganò . . .'

In a city in which the opera house was 'the focal point of the entire city,' a new composer with a reputation was obviously a figure of some importance, and certainly of great interest. Rossini arrived in the summer of 1812, and his new opera was performed for the first time on September 26. It was one of the most successful operas ever to be presented at La Scala, and ran for fifty-three nights, a record that was not beaten until 1842, when Verdi's *Nabucco* ran for fifty-eight nights. The success of *La pietra del paragone* brought Rossini the sort of fame that only an opera composer in a city like Milan could command; he was introduced into the highest circles of society, and his witty charm and good looks set him on a path of social success that would in future take up as much of his life as composing. His fame brought him more than social success, for it also bought him exemption from military service, although not, as the legend would have it, from Prince Eugène himself, who in the autumn of 1812 was battling against the Russian snows with Napoleon.

Rossini was not able to rest on his laurels for long. On November 24 the first of two further *farsè* was performed at the San Moisè, whose impresario had clearly realised that he was on to a good thing with Rossini. The second, which was produced at the end of January 1813, was called *Il signor Bruschino*, and is a more interesting and witty piece than the first. Most notable is its bizarre little overture, in which in one repeated section the string players are instructed to tap with their bows on the metal shades of the candle-holders on their music stands, an effect which may have endeared the piece to Offenbach, who revived it at the Bouffes-Parisiens in 1859. Rossini, who was living in Paris at the time, with customary diffidence and lack of interest in his own work, declined to attend.

La Fenice. The rear entrance, which had to be approached by gondola.

Before setting to work on *Il signor Bruschino*, Rossini must have been offered a commission by La Fenice, for on February 6, 1813 his *Tancredi* opened there. La Fenice was a far more important theatre than the San Moisè, and Rossini demanded a fee twice as large as he commanded for his *farsè*, which was not unreasonable, since *Tancredi* is twice as long; but having asked for 600 lire, he had to settle for 500. Rossini was not yet self-assured enough to stand out for the full amount. His financial acumen matured as he

Marietta Marcolini,
Filippo Galli and Serafino
Gentili, who all sang in
the première of *L'Italiana
in Algeri*. Galli, who
started his career as a
tenor, was making one of
his earliest appearances
as a bass. His first bass
role had been in Rossini's
Il cambiale del matrimonio.

himself matured. The librettist was Gaetano Rossi, a tiresome local hack who had provided Rossini with the libretto for *Il cambiale* and was to serve him again as librettist of *Semiramide* almost ten years later, and was still going strong in 1842, when he provided Donizetti with the libretto for *Linda di Chamounix*.

The story of *Tancredi* is from the sixteenth-century epic poet Tasso, via Voltaire, with a happy ending appended to what had originally been a tragedy to conform to the conventions of eighteenth-century *opera seria* which were still prevalent at this date. For a series of performances in Ferrara the following month Rossini attempted to return to the original tragic ending written by Voltaire, and rewrote the conclusion. The audience's characteristic reaction was to complain that such sad scenes upset their digestions.

Tancredi was the opera that made Rossini not only nationally but internationally famous, although it got off to a shaky start. The first two performances had to be stopped half way through due to the illness of the two leading ladies, and the aria from the opera which was to carry Rossini's name into every salon in Europe, and which earned in its own right a place in Byron's *Don Juan*, 'Di tanti palpiti', does not seem to have been an immediate hit. But before very long, everyone in Venice was singing the tune—so much so that, as one story has it, the public had to be reprimanded for singing it in the law courts. To modern ears the aria sounds rather less remarkable than the extraordinarily beautiful accompanied recitative which precedes it, and which has a limpid melancholy which instantly reminds one of Mozart. Nonetheless, the aria itself has a suavity and breadth of line that makes it all the more remarkable that it should supposedly have been written by Rossini in the time that it took him to boil a plate of rice for his supper, to please a demanding singer—hence its title: 'L'aria del riso', or the Rice Aria.

Yet there was no rest, for the young Rossini still had his parents to support and could not afford to slacken. After *Tancredi* in February he had to go off to Ferrara to supervise its production there, and in April he was back in Venice for a new opera to be produced at the Teatro San Benedetto, for which he was now paid 700 lire. This was *L'Italiana di Algeri*, ('The Italian girl in Algiers') the first of Rossini's operas to hold a firm place in the modern repertory. Its story was derived from the popular legend of Roxelane, the slave girl of Suleiman the Magnificent, and like Mozart's *Die Entführung aus dem Serail*, and to a lesser extent Rossini's own *La pietra del paragone*, appeals to the taste of the late eighteenth century and early nineteenth century for things oriental, and especially a fascination for Turkey. The opera has far more variety than the conventional *opera buffa*, and ranges from pure farce, via sentimental romance, to Isabella's (the 'Italian Girl' of the title) grandly mock patriotic 'Pensa alla patria', which was later cited in Rossini's defence when he was accused of not being a true Italian patriot.

After *L'Italiana* Rossini probably returned to Bologna to share his success with his family and friends there, and to enjoy a period of rest from the past hectic three years, during which he had written ten operas. His relaxation most likely took the form of sexual activity, for at this time, before he had gone prematurely bald and fat, Rossini was famous for his good looks and his sexual conquests. The better portraits show a handsome man with a lively intelligence and an ironic twinkle in the eye, a finely chiselled nose and decidedly sensual mouth. It was almost certainly during these years that he contracted the venereal disease which caused him such torments and suffering later in his life.

In December 1813 Rossini was back in Milan, where he had been commissioned to write an *opera seria* to be presented on December 26, the traditional opening night of the Carnival season, a position which carried with it much honour for the composer whose opera was chosen for the occasion. *Aureliano in Palmira* does not seem to have inspired Rossini, although he obviously thought that the overture was good enough, for he was to use it twice again. The press was scathing about the new work, and labelled it 'boring', the ultimate sin for an opera which the Milan public was condemned to hear night after night until the season ended. Its principal claim to attention is that it contains the only part that Rossini ever wrote for an already dying species, the male soprano or castrato, who had so dominated eighteenth-century opera. The singer for whom the role was written was Giovanni Velluti, one of the last great operatic castrati. Most of the later roles written for the voice were written for Velluti, including Armando in Meyerbeer's last Italian opera *Il crociatio in Egitto*. Velluti was born as late as 1780, and did not die until 1861, a few years before Rossini himself, and like Rossini, a man whose triumphs lay in some far distant past. Velluti indulged in what was then the perfectly normal practice of decorating the vocal line of the music he sang to suit his own taste and technique; but Rossini was said to have been so appalled by the result that he vowed that henceforth he would write out his vocal lines as he wanted them to be decorated himself, which may account for the increasingly florid and elaborate nature of Rossini's later vocal writing.

In April 1814 Rossini was again in Milan to receive acclamation for performances of *L'italiana*, and may have contracted to write a comic opera for La Scala, for in August 1814 *Il Turco in Italia* ('The Turk in Italy') was produced there. Its librettist was Felice Romani, certainly the best Italian librettist of the early romantic period, although he was himself by inclination a neo-classicist, an admirer of Metastasio and a friend of the finest neo-classical poet of the period, Vincenzo Monti. An influential journalist in his own right, he wrote in all some 120 librettos, including those for three of Donizetti's best known operas, and seven of Bellini's, of which the most famous are *La sonnambula* and *Norma*. He also wrote the libretto for Verdi's second, disastrous, opera *Un giorno di regno*. Romani and Rossini may have intentionally decided to follow up

Felice Romani (1788–1865). Author of over 100 opera libretti, he was only twenty-six when he supplied Rossini with the libretto for *Il Turco in Italia*. He became the most influential Italian librettist of the romantic era.

Joachim Murat (1767–1815) King of Naples, was married to Napoleon's youngest sister Caroline. Murat negotiated with the Austrians to retain his throne, but after the nationalist venture of the Rimini Declaration, was captured and shot in October 1815.

the success of *L'Italiana* with another opera about Turks and Italians, although in this case the roles of native and visitor are reversed; whether or not they did, the Milan audience, who by now had seen *L'Italiana*, clearly felt that they had been fobbed off with a second-hand piece, and a description in the *Corriere milanese* survives of the audience's reaction, with their angry shouts of '*C'est du vin de son cru*' (It's old wine in new bottles), and 'potpourri, potpourri'. Certainly it was what Stendhal used to call 'backstairs patriotism', an expression of the intense regional chauvinism from which Italy still suffered, rather than very acute critical faculties which prompted the reaction, for *Il Turco* is not in reality very similar to *L'Italiana*, either in its music or its plot, which is far more sophisticated. The Milanese did not like the idea that they were being treated as second best to Venice.

In November 1814, Rossini was back in Venice for a new opera for La Fenice. *Sigismondo* seems to have been unremarkable, and Rossini clearly knew as much himself, for he later told Hiller that its reception by the Venetian audiences had been remarkably kind. The performances of *Sigismondo* marked the beginning of a well-earned period of rest for Rossini. From now on his financial position was always potentially secure, and the time was not long away when every impresario in Italy would be vying for a new opera from him.

The months that followed *Sigismondo* may have been quiet for Rossini, but they were not so for the rest of Europe. In 1813 Napoleon had suffered a major defeat at the Battle of Leipzig, and in April 1814 had capitulated to the Allies, his dynastic and territorial ambitions having finally forced him to overreach himself. With the usual mixture of indecent haste and indifference tinged with resignation, the Italians prepared themselves for the required volte-face. 'Idiots and slaves!' Shelley fumed about a similar occasion a few years later. 'Like the frogs in the fable, because they are discontented with the log, they call upon the stork, who devours them.'

The French Imperial insignia, once so proudly displayed, was pulled down, and the Austrians set about as best they could undoing the events of the past years. They attempted to efface all traces of liberalism and nationalism, and except for the extinction of the ancient republics of Venice and Genoa, the map of Italy in 1814/15 did not differ from that of 1789. Only in the opera houses would the Italians refuse to be changed by their new masters; when the Austrians, no doubt concerned about the morality of the darkened auditorium at La Scala, tried to introduce a central chandelier, the opposition was so strong that they thought better of it.

Rossini was in Bologna in March 1815 when Napoleon escaped from Elba and began his march to Paris; Europe was caught unawares and thrown into a fluster of confusion. In Italy, all those who, like Samuel Rogers, had made haste to enjoy the freedom offered by the re-opening of Europe, fled 'like startled hares, and hurry scurry is the word'.

News of the progress of events in France was slow to reach Italy, and when it did so, was often contradictory. Allegiances were severely tested, and as the pro-French Neapolitan finance minister commented, there was in Italy 'Un peu d'espoir, et beaucoup de désespoir' (a little hope, and much despair). Napoleon's lieutenant in Naples, Joachim Murat, the husband of Napoleon's sister Caroline, who had thrown in his lot with the conquerers of his former master in 1814, decided to seize the moment and recapture Italy for Napoleon and the forces of Italian unity, and on April 5, 1815 issued his 'Rimini Declaration', a call for the Italian people to rise in his support; and then set off with his army, making his way north through the Papal States. In most places he was welcomed with enthusiasm; Bologna was no exception, and there was an armed uprising in the city in anticipation of Murat's arrival. As always on these occasions, some sort of musical celebration of the event was called for, and as the foremost composer in Bologna, Rossini set a customarily banal text by a local hydraulic engineer who fancied himself as a poet; it was one of the few occasions when Rossini showed any form of political interest, and it earned him a police record with the over-vigilant Austrian authorities. The result, *L'inno dell'independenza* ('The Hymn of Independence'), was performed in the presence of Murat on April 15; the next day the Austrians arrived back in Bologna and recaptured it, and the brief wave of nationalistic optimism was over. In June 1815, Napoleon and the French Grand Army were decisively destroyed at Waterloo, and Napoleon was sent into exile on St. Helena, from which he would never again escape to disturb the peace of Europe. The era of Napoleon was indeed over, and the era of Rossini had begun.

5

Naples. The new conqueror of Europe

Sometime in 1812 Rossini received a letter from the great dramatic coloratura soprano Isabella Colbran, whom he had almost certainly met in Milan that year. The letter may well have been requesting him to write a role for her, and this would have meant going to Naples, where she was the reigning *prima donna* at the San Carlo. Rossini was busy at the time, but Colbran would almost certainly have tried to persuade the manager of the San Carlo, Domenico Barbaja, to get Rossini to come to Naples. After the success of *Tancredi* and *L'Italiana*, Barbaja would have taken little persuading.

Domenico Barbaja was one of the most colourful and influential figures of the early nineteenth-century operatic world, one of those people with whom show business is all too often cursed and all too seldom blessed. Born in 1778, he started life as a café waiter in Milan. Later described by Rossini's second wife Olympe as having an excellent heart, 'but no sort of education' (she was hardly one to speak herself), 'he had,' as Stendhal puts it, 'and still has, a good eye for the main chance,' and as a waiter, seized the opportunity to invent a hot drink which is still popular in Italy and Vienna under the name 'granita di cafè', but which was once called a 'barbajata'. From being a waiter, Barbaja moved to running the gaming tables at La Scala, where he had a virtual monopoly for the whole city. There were always large numbers of French troops stationed in Milan, and Barbaja seems also to have speculated in army contracts, and by whatever means, soon accumulated a large fortune.

In 1809 he moved to Naples, with a contract as chief impresario for the city, giving him control over not only the San Carlo, but also the Teatro del Fondo and the Teatro dei Fiorentini. As in Milan, he also secured a licence to operate the gaming tables; he did well to move from Milan, for in 1815 the Austrians closed down the gaming tables at La Scala. Barbaja's energy was immense: not only did he eventually capture Rossini for Naples, but he also established Rossini's two most important successors in Italy, Bellini and Donizetti, and discovered the greatest dancer of the age, Maria Taglioni, and one of the greatest singers, Giuditta Pasta. As if this was not enough, in 1815 he undertook the contract for the building of the new church which King Ferdinand founded to mark the restoration of the Bourbon dynasty, San Francesco di Paola, and the following year, when the San Carlo was destroyed by fire, Barbaja ensured that it was rebuilt in less than a year, an

Domenico Barbaja (1778–1841). In the background of the painting can be seen the figures of Rossini, Bellini, and Giuditta Pasta, artists with whose careers Barbaja was closely associated.

almost incredible feat. During a period in Vienna in the 1820s, when he was Manager of the Kärntnertortheater, he was responsible for commissioning Weber's *Euryanthe* and Schubert's *Fierrabras*.

Such was the man with whom, in the spring of 1815, Rossini signed an agreement in which he was to act as musical director at the two most important theatres under Barbaja's management, for which he was also to write two new operas a year. Rossini was shrewd enough to ensure for himself a vital escape clause that he should be allowed to write operas elsewhere if he so desired, but in all other respects he was tied to Barbaja and Naples, and later commented that, if Barbaja had been able to, he would have made him run the theatre kitchens too. And yet it was a fruitful bond, for it provided Rossini with a stable and secure base which gave him freedom to develop as an opera composer, away from the pressures which were imposed by the life of an unattached composer, subject to the more limiting demands of commercialism.

Rossini's arrival in Naples in 1815 coincided with the

47

The Return of King Ferdinand to Naples. 1815. A contemporary painting of the scene. Ferdinand was said to have been delighted with the lavish Empire style decoration carried out in his palaces by Queen Caroline Murat

restoration of the Bourbon King Ferdinand I and IV to the throne of the Two Sicilies, of which Naples was the capital. The Naples of the pre-Napoleonic period was the second largest city in Europe, and the most densely populated; it was also one of the poorest and most backward cities in Europe. The Napoleonic reforms of Joseph Bonaparte and Joachim Murat had done much to clear away the worst abuses, but the return of King Ferdinand after such a long period in exile could not but be regarded by many with apprehension, especially after the fearsome reprisals that had been taken on the first restoration of the King in 1799. King Ferdinand was not the man to appreciate the political tensions of post-Napoleonic Europe. He was barely literate, and often gross and coarse in his manner; his favourite activity was hunting, and he was often described as having the appearance of some country squire. Most of the political events of his reign had been dominated by his wife Queen Caroline, daughter of the Austrian Empress Maria-Theresa and sister of the executed Queen of France Marie-Antoinette; she had died in exile in 1814, and until his death in 1825, King Ferdinand ruled alone.

The seven years that coincide with Rossini's stay in Naples were a period of political uncertainty, dominated as in most countries in Europe, by the conflict between those who wished to return to the old order of things and those who wished to proceed along the lines laid down by Napoleon. In Naples the issue was fought over the King's refusal to agree to the Liberals' demands for a democratic Constitution similar to that granted in 1812 to the Spanish, and it

48

led to the growth of an underground revolutionary movement, the Carbonari, and eventually, in 1820, to a revolution.

Rossini's arrival in Naples also coincided with the reopening of Europe to English travellers, who poured across the channel in droves, for the first time since 1803, like prisoners let out of gaol.

Naples always had been, and still was, the main destination for the English traveller in Europe, and after 1814/15 it became once again the winter home for a significant section of English society, including, in 1815, the Princess of Wales. Stendhal observed drily of a ball at the royal palace in 1817 that 'all London was present', and indeed for Stendhal, as for many people, Naples was the only city in Italy which could claim to be a truly cosmopolitan capital city. Comparing Naples society to that of Paris, he decided that in Naples it was 'perhaps livelier, and assuredly noisier'. Naples had a flourishing indigenous social and intellectual life, which included two renowned salons to which every visitor endeavoured to secure an introduction, those of the Marchese di Berio and the

The Bay of Naples. A contemporary print, showing Vesuvius smoking in the background.

Archbishop of Taranto. By 1815 the Archbishop was an old man of seventy-one, and virtually a national monument. 'When you come to Naples,' wrote Prince Henry of Prussia, 'you must see Pompeii, Vesuvius, and the Archbishop of Taranto.' Samuel Rogers, who did so in 1814, found the Archbishop courteous and civilised, and surrounded by his famous cats. The Marchese di Berio was an Anglophile, a devotee of Byron, and a friend and patron of the greatest sculptor of the age, Canova. Lady Morgan visited Berio's salon in 1820, and found the Marchese writing an ode to Byron; the guests included Gabriel Rossetti, father of the poet and painter Dante Gabriel Rossetti, who was famed as an 'improvisatore', or declaimer of improvised verse, and Rossini himself, who provided the musical entertainment, accompanying himself and Isabella Colbran at the piano.

Naples appealed to visitors because in some way it contained in microcosm everything that people from the cold and cheerless north of Europe found most attractive about Italy. They delighted in its spectacular natural setting, with the great sweep of the bay dominated by Vesuvius smoking in the distance (the volcano's most recent eruption had been in 1814, and it remained active until the next eruption in 1822). The appalling poverty (there were estimated to be 150,000 'lazzaroni', the vagrants and beggars who crowded the streets of the city, out of a total population of half a million) seems not to have disturbed people, for as so often, the sun tinged poverty with the picturesque. Samuel Rogers, whose journal only includes a passing reference to a dead lazzarone found one morning on the steps of an English lady's house, wrote of the lazzaroni: 'They seem to be a noisy, gay and harmless race. Their principal luxuries are macaroni and iced waters,' whilst Lady Blessington concluded: 'Who that has seen Naples, can wonder that her children are idle and luxuriously disposed.' It needs a Dickens to remind us of the other side of the picture: 'But, lovers and hunters of the picturesque,' he warns, 'let us not keep too studiously out of view the miserable depravity, degradation and wretchedness, with which this gay Neapolitan life is inseparably associated.'

Nonetheless, the streets of Naples were famous for their teeming activity; 'The streets of Naples present daily the appearance of a fête,' wrote Lady Blessington, and those who wandered in the Strada Nuova and the Mole were captivated by the endless street entertainments: 'filosofi', reciters of Tasso to appreciative crowds, much to the surprise of English travellers; the musicians and singers; the conjurers and mountebanks demonstrating some magnetic trick or patent remedy; the sellers of water-ices; the puppet booths and the commedia dell'arte troups which Samuel Rogers observed outside the Teatro del Fondo, confirming a taste for popular theatre shared by even the King, dubbed 'il re lazzarone' by his subjects. The activity did not cease at sunset: 'The gaiety of the streets of Naples at night is unparalleled,' wrote Lady Blessington, 'The sounds of guitars were heard mingling with the joyous laughs of the lazzaroni . . . Groups of three or four persons, with guitars, were seen seated on a terrace, or on a bench before their houses singing Neapolitan airs, and barcaroles [sic], in a style that would not have offended the ears of Rossini himself'.

It was probably this innate musicality of its people that led to the reputation of Naples as one of the most lively, and indeed most important, musical centres in Europe. A whole string of eighteenth-century composers had worked in the city: Alessandro Scarlatti, Stradella, Pergolesi, Jommelli, Paisiello, and Cimarosa all belonged to the Neapolitan school, and both Piccini and Spontini were brought up there. In 1769 De la Lande described Naples as 'the principal source of music'. Above all, it was in opera that Naples considered itself pre-eminent; *opera buffa*, the Italian comic opera, was created in Naples (the first opera to be classified an *opera buffa* appeared at the Teatro dei Fiorentini, a theatre with which Rossini was to be associated, in 1709).

In 1782, the English Dr Moore wrote: 'Naples is celebrated for its opera, which is considered the best in Europe,' and it was to keep this reputation for some time to come. Musical standards were certainly higher at the San Carlo than elsewhere in Italy, and Berlioz wrote in his memoirs that, upon arriving in Naples, 'for the first time since coming to Italy, I heard music'. Even so, Berlioz noted that in the orchestra there were too few cellos, and both he and Mendelssohn observed that the first violinist, who did duty as conductor, had to tap with his bow to keep the orchestra in time. The chorus too was weak, and the soprano and tenor lines often had to be written in unison, since each was unable to hold a single line. Nonetheless, even Berlioz praised the 'zest, fire and brio' of performances in Naples, especially of *opera buffa* at the Teatro del Fondo, which had for some time presented a formidable rival to the San Carlo, and Stendhal too praised the precision and attack of the orchestra at the San Carlo. Only the stage production and decor were disappointing; Stendhal describes one performance at which the scenery was so constructed that the feet of the chorus could be seen protruding below the bottom of the flats, and illusionism of the kind developed by Sanquirico at La Scala was never pursued. Spohr, at the San Carlo in 1817, recalled a curious custom demanded by court etiquette which further inhibited attempts at creating theatrical illusionism: 'It is required that the curtain be raised upon the King's arrival in his box, placing the poor singers in the unhappy position of having to stand and be looked at during the playing of the overture.'

The last heirs of the eighteenth-century operatic tradition were still living in Naples, but Rossini arrived at an opportune moment. Two of the most popular of the eighteenth-century composers, Cimarosa and Paisiello, had fallen foul of the kaleidoscopic political changes that had taken place between 1797 and 1815— Cimarosa, believed to have been imprisoned and then exiled to

51

Venice for his Republican sympathies, died in 1801, whilst Paisiello, the former favourite of the Bourbon régime, although still living, was in disgrace for his acceptance of Napeoleon's patronage, and died the year after Rossini's arrival. Paisiello had once called Rossini 'a licentious composer', but despite the reputation that Naples had for being what the French opera composer Hérold called in 1814 'the land of Cabal', Rossini's only important opponent was Zingarelli, the director of the Royal School of Music, who was said to have forbidden his pupils even to read the scores of Rossini's operas, let alone attend performances; legend has it that Sigismondo, the librarian of the Royal School, used to hide Rossini's scores away on a top shelf, out of the reach of curious students. But if it is true that Zingarelli told Spohr that if Mozart had studied more he might have written a good opera, then Rossini had little to fear from the opposition; and anyway, his success depended upon the Neapolitan public, not upon a behind-the-times composer like Zingarelli.

Rossini's first opera for the San Carlo was *Elisabetta, regina d'Inghilterra* (Elizabeth, Queen of England), the story derived from an eighteenth-century English novel, via a play seen in Naples the previous year, about Queen Elizabeth I's supposed love for the Earl of Leicester. (It was not, as is often suggested, taken from Scott's *Kenilworth*, which was not published until 1821). The title role was written for Isabella Colbran, whose name was to be

Isabella Colbran (1785–1845). A portrait by Heinrich Schmitt of the Spanish-born soprano showing her in the role of Saffo in Mayr's opera of that name. 1817.

closely linked with Rossini's during the Naples years, and whom he eventually married. Colbran was Spanish, and in 1815 was thirty years old. Stendhal has left us a description of Colbran: 'Hers was beauty of a most queenly kind: noble features which on stage radiated majesty; an eye like that of a Circassian maiden darting fire; and to crown it all, a true and deep instinct for tragedy.' Unfortunately, for complex political reasons, Stendhal disliked Colbran, and could not resist a final characteristic put-down: 'Off-stage she possessed about as much dignity as the average milliner's assistant.' Her voice was what we would call today a dramatic coloratura soprano, with, as one contemporary critic described it, 'smoothness, strength, and prodigious extension of tones; from the bass G to the high F, that is, for almost three octaves, it makes itself heard in a progression always even in mellowness and energy'. Spohr, who heard her sing Elisabetta in 1817, wrote that 'She is rather inferior to Catalani in voice, and lacks her mechanical perfection, but sings with true feeling and acts with passion'. This was the voice and personality for whom Rossini wrote many of his greatest roles.

Elisabetta is an *opera seria*. 'Opera seria' means quite simply 'serious opera', but during the eighteenth century a whole set of conventions and formalities had become established, many of which were still in operation at the beginning of the nineteenth century. *Opera seria* mirrored the static, hierarchic ideals of the eighteenth century; it was a drama of statement and reflection rather than of conflict, as is apparent in its conventions. The important parts were all written for sopranos (male or female) and tenors. There were only minor parts for basses, very rarely at all for baritones, and for mezzo-sopranos usually only when they appeared in breeches roles. The range of vocal characterisation available to the composer was therefore extremely limited, as were the opportunities for dramatic conflict between characters based on vocal contrast. This was accentuated by the convention whereby the action progressed through rapidly sung recitative, whilst the main musical content lay in arias in which dramatic expression was achieved through the contrast of fast and slow sections, and vocal display. There were only rarely ensembles in which more than one person sang, and choruses played only a very minor role. As we have seen, *opere serie* were not expected to have sad endings, in accord with the rational optimism of the eighteenth century.

These were the conventions within which Rossini had to work. They were increasingly inappropriate to the sensibility of a post revolutionary Italy just beginning to come to terms with emergent Romanticism and Nationalism. Composers in other countries in Europe escaped their deadening effect by drawing on other traditions and sources, but Rossini helped to push Italian opera into the age of Romanticism from within, gradually breaking down the conventions, or stretching them so that they became unrecognisable. The process is already apparent in *Elisabetta*, an early example of an opera based on a typically romantic theme, a story from English history. The main parts are still written for sopranos and tenors, and the vocal writing is if anything more florid, but *recitativo secco*, recitative accompanied by harpsichord, is abandoned in favour of a more unified orchestral accompaniment throughout, a step which composers like Paisiello and Mayr had taken previously, no doubt influenced by the example of French opera, but which Rossini developed consistently to create a more integrated form. The formal pattern of the arias is extended and opened out so that the traditional slow and fast sections are often motivated by some intervening dramatic incident, rather than following straight on from each other. Ensembles are expanded to contain dramatic progress rather than just static expression, and the chorus plays an increasingly important part in the action. Again, none of these innovations can be attributed to Rossini alone but in his hand they led to the development of a vehicle which Donizetti and Bellini found capable of sustaining the ideals of Romanticism in opera, and which continued to be viable until Verdi in his turn found the form conventionalised and stultifying.

Elisabetta opened on October 4, 1815, a state occasion at which the king and his family were present. It was a success, and converted all but the most hardened of the old school in Naples, although even these were forced to acknowledge Rossini's conquest of the San Carlo. Rossini himself did not linger long in Naples; there remained one city which he had yet to conquer with a new opera, Rome, for which he set out soon after *Elisabetta* had opened.

6

Rome. *The Barber of Seville*

Rome was in all respects different from Naples, and the differences became apparent to the traveller long before he had reached the city itself. Spohr, travelling from the north in 1816, was immediately struck by the difference between the fertile land of the north and the barren, brigand-infested country of the Roman campagna: 'The route was tedious, with neither houses nor trees, nor any other sights save those sorry monuments to Roman justice, the long poles on which are hung the arms and legs of robbers and murderers.'

Once the city was reached, the picture was not much happier; Stendhal, comparing it with Naples as Rossini must have done, wrote: 'Here, all is decadent, all is memory, all is dead; effort is unknown, energy without purpose, nothing moves with haste.' The great classical monuments lay still half-unrevealed, a prey to the over-enthusiastic amateur excavators and the flocks of sheep and pigs which wandered over the semi-rural, overgrown ruins of the Forum. Some found it picturesque, as Shelley when

Shelley in Rome. A posthumous portrait by Joseph Severn. Shelley was in Rome in 1819, and wrote much of *Prometheus Unbound* there.

Joseph Woodhead, his wife Harriet and her brother Henry Comber, 1816. A portrait drawing by Ingres (1780–1867) of one of the numerous English families who flocked to Rome after the opening of Europe to English travellers.

describing the Colosseum 'overgrown by the wild olive, the myrtle and the fig tree, and threaded by little paths which wind among its ruined stairs and immeasurable galleries,' whilst others more sententious took the occasion to draw a moral, like the painter Henry Sass, who described how, 'The Forum, of Rome, where the intellect of the world was concentrated, the seat of universal empire, is converted into a cattle market, with the contemptible designation of Campo Vaccino; and the walks of philosophers covered with asses, monks, and straw. Such is the mutability of human affairs'. Lady Morgan, as usual, bemoaned the loss of 'the only man and government which could have redeemed her from sloth, filth and inertness,' and indeed all the most recent improvements to the city—the creation of the Piazza del Popolo, the restoration of the Pantheon—were due to the obsessive activity of Napoleon. Even so, large areas of the city were decayed and unhealthy, and Lady Morgan described the avenue of St John Lateran as having 'no parallel in the history of desolation. In this spot the malaria reigns undisputed'.

Its disease ridden setting meant that visitors came to the city only in the winter, but during these months Rome became, despite its gloomy appearance, the cosmopolitan centre for 'a congress of talent assembled from nations of the earth, to promote the arts'. Here France, Austria, and Russia had established academies of art, and the city was teeming with foreign students. At the French Ecole de Rome was Ingres, earning his living with exquisite pencil portrait drawings, many of them recording some of the multitude of English visitors in Rome, described by Byron

Rome (*right and opposite*). Two contemporary prints showing the decayed state of the city in 1815, despite the attempts of Napoleon to restore some of its former grandeur.

as: 'A parcel of staring boobies, who go about gaping and wishing to be at once cheap and magnificent.' Here in 1815 the curious could visit the sculptor Canova's studio, and then compare his work in progress with that of his greatest rival, the Danish sculptor Thorwaldsen, who had been in Rome since 1797. In Rome too were gathered the remnants of Napoleon's family, who were visited with fascination and awe, like caged wild animals, by the tourists who came to the city: his formidable mother, Madame Mère, his uncle Cardinal Fesch, his brothers Louis (ex-King of Holland, and father of the future Napoleon III) and Lucien; his sisters Caroline Murat (ex-Queen of Naples) and Pauline Borghese, who so shocked people when she posed naked for Canova, and at whose famous Friday-evening concerts Rossini used to give his famous rendition of 'Largo al factotum', and Lady Morgan heard Ester Mombelli sing. Of English society in the winter of 1815/16, the visitor would have found, amongst many others, the Duchess of Devonshire, devoted admirer and friend of Cardinal Consalvi and a keen amateur excavator, and Lord and Lady Holland, the leaders of Whig society in London.

Rome was the capital of the state ruled by the Pope, Pius VII, who had been elected at the Conclave held in Venice in 1800, and had suffered the ignominy of being imprisoned and then exiled from Rome in 1809. Pius returned to his seat in 1815, but the real ruler of Rome was his Secretary of State, Cardinal Consalvi, a career churchman who never took holy orders, and whom Stendhal described as 'the foremost statesman in Europe'. It was Consalvi who had negotiated the Napoleonic Concordat of 1801,

Pauline Borghese. A sculpture by Canova (1757–1822). Pauline, who was notoriously flighty, was the only member of Napoleon's family to stand by him after his downfall.

and who later negotiated for the Papacy at the Congress of Vienna, which met in 1815 to carve up post-Napoleonic Europe. Although no liberal, he was a pragmatic enough statesman to realise that the events of the revolutionary and Napoleonic era could not be simply ignored, and attempted, often facing much opposition from his fellow Cardinals, to restore a firmer but more flexible form of government. In particular, he abolished some of the more bizarrely mediaeval practices that were still in operation, such as the tradition of signalling the start of the Carnival with the execution of a prisoner, and he also attempted to deal with the appalling problem of the brigands who haunted the outlying areas of the city, often in such numbers that the inhabitants were virtually besieged within the city. But Consalvi notwithstanding, the Papal régime was an oppressive one; Lady Morgan described it as the most military government in Europe. Censorship, for example, was oppressive in a way that only a beleaguered system finds necessary; the eighteenth-century Philosophes were still banned, as Stendhal found to his fury when his copy of Montesquieu was confiscated at the Roman border, and arguments which Lady Morgan found were being used by the Church to counter modern developments in scientific thought were the same as those that had been used against Galileo 300 years previously.

Nowhere was the anomalous position of the Papal government clearer than in its dealings with the theatre. Consalvi himself was one of the most artistically enlightened men of his age; a friend of Cimarosa, he was said to have attended rehearsals of Cimarosa's

58

Cardinal Consalvi (1757–1824) presenting the figures of Romagna, Pontecorvo, Benevento and the Marches to Pius VII under the auspices of Austria, 1815. A contemporary print celebrating Consalvi's success at the Congress of Vienna.

operas in Rome to ensure that the correct tempi were being observed, and he always took a keen interest in the activities of the Roman opera houses. And yet, officially the Papal government did not recognise the existence of theatres in the city at all; they were legally designated as temporary structures, and for this reason were always built of wood, which meant that they had an extremely insalubrious reputation, as well as being a perpetual fire-risk. As Lady Morgan wrote:

The theatres of Rome, in consequence of the modified toleration under which they exist, are dark, dirty, and paltry in their decorations; but what is infinitely worse, they are so offensive to the senses, so disgusting in the details of their arrangement, that to particularise would be impossible; suffice to say, that the corridors of the Argentina exemplify the nastiness of the Roman habits and manners more forcibly than volumes could describe.

The Teatro della Torre Argentina, normally the home of *opera seria* in Rome, was where *Il barbiere di Siviglia* received its première. Of the Teatro Valle, where Rossini's first opera for Rome was produced, Lady Morgan's comment is brief and to the point: 'A very small, mean, and dirty theatre.' In 1815, the authorities commissioned a report on the state of the Roman theatres which described their 'discomfort and filth', but nothing was done about it, and on the whole their attitude was the same as

59

Louis Spohr (1784–1859)
Violin virtuoso and
composer. His memoirs,
which contain an account
of his travels in Italy
between 1815 and 1817,
provide a lively account
of musical practice in
Italy during these years.

that stated in a reply to a petition from the citizens of Rome for leave to repair their theatres, that Rome was for churches and not for theatres.

The artistic standards in these theatres seem to have been as poor as the buildings themselves. Stendhal attended a performance of *Tancredi* at the Teatro Argentina which he said would have been booed off the stage in Brescia or Bologna, and when the Shelleys visited the opera in Rome in 1818, Shelley described it as: 'The worst I ever saw.' The orchestral players for opera were all amateurs, and Rossini did not know whether to be more appalled that his barber played the clarinet in the orchestra of the Teatro Valle, or that his clarinettist also turned out to be his barber. Fifteen years later, Berlioz, who called Rome an 'anti-musical city', found the situation at the Valle unchanged; there was only one cello in the orchestra, and he was a goldsmith by profession. Mendelssohn, in Rome at the same time as Berlioz, described the Roman orchestras as being: 'worse than anyone can imagine; both musicians and the right feeling for music are wanting. The few violinists play according to their individual tastes, and make their entrances as and when they please,' an observation confirmed by Spohr, who described how: 'Every one of them plays ornaments as it takes his fancy, and turns on almost every note, so that the ensemble sounds more like the din an orchestra makes when it is warming up and tuning than harmonious music.' Of the standards of staging the descriptions are just as depressing. Kotzebue, who brought a man of the theatre's eye to these things, describes how the performers were in the habit of making holes in the curtains so that they could look into the audience from behind them, a practice familiar to present-day devotees of amateur theatricals, and at the Teatro Valle, the holes were so big that: '. . . not only the head, but almost the whole body could be conveniently thrust through.' His description of a performance at the Teatro Apollo, another theatre with which Rossini was to be associated, in 1806 is almost too hilarious to be believable:

At the theatre of Apollo, a drama full of horror was given: the scene was a forest at night, and the lamps, of course, were let down; but the moment the chief actress, who was probably thought handsome, appeared on the stage, the audience cried out 'Lumi, lumi' (Lights, lights), upon which the lamps immediately re-appeared; but the smoke arising from them was very great, and the audience grew impatient. The candle-snuffers now appeared on the stage, and trimmed the lamps during the representation: but as they did not burn well, the audience cried out again, 'Lumi, lumi', and two dirty looking fellows came forth, carrying boxes filled with candles, which they placed on the stage. During all this the actors proceeded as if nothing had happened.

Spohr wrote resignedly:

One is accustomed to hearing one of the principal characters sing for a quarter of an hour at the most climactic moment, while the others

Teatro Argentina, Rome. Originally built in 1732, the present façade dates from 1826. The theatre's name has nothing to do with the South American country, but derives from the fact that it was built near the palace of a Bishop of Strasbourg, the Torre Argentina (Argentoratum being the Roman name for Strasbourg).

promenade in the background, or talk and joke with their colleagues in the wings.

In late October or November 1815, Rossini made the journey to Rome to supervise a production of his *Il Turco in Italia* at the Teatro Valle, and to write a new opera for that theatre called *Torvaldo e Dorliska*, which was performed on the opening night of the Carnival season, December 26. Rossini sent the customary sign to his mother that the opera had not been a success, a drawing of a flask, for which the Italian word is 'fiasco'.

On December 15, whilst in the thick of rehearsals for *Torvaldo*, Rossini signed a contract with the Duke Francesco Sforza Cesarini for an opera to be performed at the Nobile Teatro della Torre Argentina, which was the theatre that had been allocated by Consalvi for the 1816 season of *opera buffa* in Rome (*opera buffa* usually took place at the Teatro Valle). The Argentina stood on land owned by the Cesarini family, and the Duke had decided to try his hand at theatre management in 1807; unfortunately, he did not make a great success of it, and by 1815 was heavily in debt; contracting Rossini was his last attempt to gain financial solvency.

The genesis of the opera that was to become *Il barbiere di Siviglia* was beset with more than the usual fair share of misfortunes and disasters. Although Rossini had signed the contract on December 15, and the first performance was scheduled for February 20, 1816, there was still no libretto by January 17, for the original librettist, Jacopo Ferretti, had produced a libretto with which the Duke was dissatisfied, and since so much was at stake, he dared not take any risks. A new librettist was hastily found and signed up, Cesare Sterbini the librettist of the recent *Torvaldo e Dorliska*, who undertook to deliver the first act by January 25, a week later, and the second act four days after that on January 29. Rossini delivered the music of the first act for copying on February 6. Then on February 7, the Duke suddenly died, aged only forty-four, having been stricken by a chill caught in his own theatre, about whose icy cold he had complained to no less a person than Consalvi a few days previously. The Duchess and the late Duke's agent immediately took over the running of the theatre, for a lot of money was tied up in the forthcoming season. The problems did not cease there, however. The libretto put together by Sterbini was an adaptation of Beaumarchais's play *Le Barbier de Seville*, the story of how the young Count Almaviva, aided by the invaluable barber Figaro, manages to abduct the beautiful Rosina from under the watchful eye of her jealous guardian Dr Bartolo. It was in many ways an ideal choice, for Beaumarchais had himself conceived it as a comic opera, and had furnished it with songs. But it had the disadvantage that it had been set previously by Paisiello, and as such had provided the basis for one of the most popular of all his operas. To avoid raising odious comparisons, Rossini and his librettist actually gave the opera the title *Almaviva, ossia La precauzione inutile* ('Almaviva, or the Useless Precautions'), and in the printed libretto published a 'Notice to the public', which restated the composer's 'respect and veneration for the immortal composer who preceded him'. Rossini later recalled that he had written to Paisiello himself, reiterating his desire not to offend the older master.

'Inutile precauzione' indeed! Despite the fine line-up of singers for the first performance, which included the famous Spanish tenor Garcia in the role of Almaviva, the opening was a monumental fiasco, and *Il barbiere* joined the ranks of those operas which, like *La traviata* and *Carmen* later, were condemned at their first performance before being accepted as masterpieces. The audience contained two factions hostile to the opera: the supporters of Paisiello, and the regulars of the Teatro Valle, annoyed at having to move from their favourite haunt to the Argentina. Into this hostile atmosphere stepped Rossini, wearing a curious Spanish-style outfit with gold buttons that had been given to him for the occasion by Barbaja, and which attracted

Geltrude Righetti-Giorgi (1793–1862). A childhood friend of Rossini's, she came out of temporary retirement to appear in *Il barbiere*, and became as a result, as Spohr put it, 'the darling of the Carnival.'

instant derision from the audience. Things went from bad to worse; the Rosina, Geltrude Righetti-Giorgi, was whistled at her first entrance, and it is from her account that we know about what happened next. The singer playing Bartolo tripped over a trapdoor as he entered, and spent the whole of his first aria trying to staunch the flow of blood from his nose; as if this was not enough, a cat appeared on stage 'during the superb finale, mixing amongst the performers. The excellent Figaro, Zamboni, chased it off one side; it returned from the other, and hurled itself into the arms of Bartolo; the charitable audience called out to it, imitated its miaowing, and encouraged it by voice and gesture to proceed with its improvised role'. There would be few audiences in the world capable of showing self restraint at such goings on even if they wanted to; the audience that night had no intention of doing so.

The reports of Rossini's reaction to the events are conflicting; some say that he went straight home and took to his bed because he was so upset, whilst Righetti-Giorgi says that he simply went to bed because he was quite indifferent to the reception his works had received. What we know of Rossini's hypersensitivity would conform with the first report, but equally, he always retained a curious detachment towards his own works, and several reports confirm that at the end of the performance Rossini, as if in defiance of the audience, very ostentatiously stood and applauded his performers amidst the catcalls and whistling. Whatever Rossini's reaction, he did not have to suffer long, for on the second performance the audience changed its mind and recognised the true worth of the new opera. *The Barber* claimed its deserved success.

It is worth lingering over *The Barber* a little longer, for the very good reason that it is Rossini's best and most famous opera. It is his best opera not because it contains better music than any of his others, nor because it shows any greater dramatic skill, but quite simply because it has the best libretto that Rossini ever set. One might go so far as to say that an opera is only as good as its libretto, and certainly *The Barber* might be cited as evidence if the validity of such a rule were to be put to the test. Beaumarchais's play could not be more suitable, for as has been shown, Beaumarchais was himself a musician, and had envisaged the play as a comic opera with spoken dialogue. Its roots lie deep in the fertile soil of *commedia dell'arte*, the ancient Italian popular theatre, with its stock of easily recognized characters and simple plot outlines, within which had developed a rich improvisatory acting style. In France the tradition was adapted by Molière in the seventeenth century, and by Marivaux and Beaumarchais in the eighteenth, although all three French dramatists achieved a far greater sophistication and subtlety than was ever seen in the Italian original. In Italy in the eighteenth century both Gozzi and Goldoni played with the tradition in different ways, but it was above all in Italian *opera buffa* that it survived into the nineteenth century, and

Rossini c1815. A portrait
by Vincenzo Camuccini.

Rossini's *Barber* therefore represents a meeting of the separate strands of the *commedia* tradition. The parentage of the characters in *The Barber* can be quite clearly traced back to the *commedia dell'arte*; there are many characteristics of Pantalone to be found in Dr Bartolo, and of Brighella and Arlecchino in Figaro, and the story itself is derived from an archetypal *commedia* plot. Furthermore, like *commedia dell'arte*, *opera buffa* was a popular art form, and there was considerable cross fertilisation. At a performance of an *opera buffa* which he attended in Naples, Stendhal noted that the part of a servant was played by a popular actor rather than a singer, and his description of the action makes it clear that it was very close to the classic style of the *commedia dell'arte*, with its use of '*lazze*', or semi-improvised comic routines. Goldoni wrote many *opera buffa* librettos, and at the first performance of *The Barber* Goldoni's one-act play *Il ventaglio* was played in the interval. Thus, both by descent via Beaumarchais and the traditions of *opera buffa*, and by its contact with the popular theatre of the day, Rossini's *Barber* derives its enduring strength and popularity from a rich vein of theatrical history. It is interesting that Paisiello's version, which is even more faithful to Beaumarchais's text, shows much less evidence of the popular tradition; Paisiello, like Cimarosa, aiming for an international audience, wrote in a more superficially sophisticated style. Rossini, with more modest pretensions, has survived, Paisiello has not.

Because Mozart, in *Le Nozze di Figaro*, and Rossini both wrote operas based on plays by Beaumarchais, comparisons are inevitable and often arise. But they are really only useful in so far as they highlight the merits rather than the supposed limitations of Rossini's opera. Although technically they are both Italian *opere buffe*, and from Beaumarchais share the same characters (although Mozart's, written thirty years before Rossini's, deals with a later stage in the Figaro-Almaviva story) they derive from quite different theatrical traditions. Rossini's opera, as we have seen, derives its strength from the lively popular tradition of the age, while Mozart's *Figaro* belongs to a more courtly, sophisticated tradition. For the composers of Mozart's Vienna, the popular tradition was to be found not in Italian *opera buffa* but in the German *Singspiel*, to which Mozart himself contributed *Die Entführung aus dem Serail* and *Die Zauberflöte*. Hence the robust and lively humour of Rossini's score in contrast to the wider ranging and more deeply felt sentiments of Mozart's. Commentators often talk about Rossini's zest and brio, and here again comparison with Mozart is useful, for in many ways, Rossini's operas have a curiously static quality; much use is made (often to comic effect) of grand musical periods, and the drama tends to progress in clearly defined sections, with a stop/start motion. Rossini had less of Mozart's ability to capture the myriad fleeting changes of pace and mood of a comedy, those moments of frenzied energy, those sudden moments of sadness, of amazed stupefaction or simple chaos that are intertwined in miraculously extended sequences. On the other hand, no composer, not even Mozart, had Rossini's sense of purely musical (as opposed to dramatic) wit, and it is a wit that derives, paradoxically for an Italian composer, not primarily from the vocal writing, but from never flagging orchestral invention. Rossini's greatest arias derive their genius not from their tunes but from their marvellous accompaniments: Figaro's entrance aria 'Largo al factotum' in *The Barber* achieves its manic effect through its tireless orchestral support, which never seems to allow the singer to draw breath; Basilio's 'Calumny' aria achieves its effect through the great orchestral crescendo which, with its nervous beginning that grows into an outrageous climax, portrays marvellously, in purely musical terms, the effect of a little calumny whispered in a receptive ear and growing to stupendous proportions. Of all composers, perhaps only Verdi, who was one of the many who admired *The Barber*, was able to capture this same effortless musical wit in his *Falstaff*.

We should not be surprised that Rossini chose to set a text which had already been set. Few operas at that date used texts which had not been set before in some form or another, and had Sterbini and Rossini but known it, Paisiello had no particular claim on *Le Barbier de Séville*; between the publication of Beaumarchais's play in 1775 and Paisiello's version in 1782 there were two operatic settings, and between 1782 and 1816 a further three. The fact is that at this date operas were only rarely written to entirely original librettos. There are several reasons for this: one is that audiences clearly liked familiar stories. Stendhal believed that, in accord with his general theory of Italian opera, this was because of the Italians' generally arrested intellectual growth; but in fact the reason was much more straightforward. It will be recalled that opera audiences paid scant attention to what went on on stage, only ceasing the hubbub of noise when a favourite singer appeared or a popular number was reached. 'In such a state of things,' wrote Antonio Gallenga, 'it may be understood, that no great justice can be paid to the poet's abilities. The libretto-maker is generally an uneducated wretch, who sells his works for a few crowns apiece'.

If the audience was to have any idea of what was going on when it did pay attention, it was obviously desirable that the story and characters should be familiar. Printed copies of the libretto were always sold at a performance, and Stendhal tells us that it was customary for people to peruse it beforehand. Even so, one can be fairly sure that when a text was set which had not previously been seen as an opera, it had already enjoyed a success in the theatre as a play; Rossini's *Elisabetta* and *La gazza ladra* were both based on recently performed plays, the latter derived from a French boulevard play, an especially popular source for Italian librettos, and one from which a librettist like Felice Romani often borrowed direct, without waiting for an Italian version to appear on stage; in

A page of the autograph score of *Il barbiere* showing the orchestral introduction to 'Largo al factotum.'

1833 he is found writing fretfully that he is awaiting a shipment of plays from Paris for ideas for a new libretto for Bellini.

The frantic haste with which all operas were thrown together at this time is another reason for the use of second-hand librettos. Sterbini almost certainly had the Paisiello libretto to hand when preparing his own for Rossini, and in the days before the laws of copyright there was little to prevent direct borrowing. Also, few librettists of that era were competent dramatists or writers in their own right. A quick survey of Rossini's librettists will soon show us what an Italian composer could expect at this period. Gaetano Rossi, the Venetian librettist of *Il cambiale, Tancredi* and *Semiramide* was typical of a whole breed of mediocre hacks who hung around picking up work wherever they could, adapting librettos, writing occasional verses for special events, or texts for cantatas and celebrations. Often a librettist was more permanently attached to an opera house, and could rely upon a steady demand for his work; such was Luigi Romanelli, the librettist of *La pietra del paragone*, who wrote an enormous number of librettos for La Scala; and in Naples, the ubiquitous Tottola and Schmitt, librettists in the pay of Barbaja. Another breed was the aristocratic dilettante who fancied himself as an author: Conte Francesco Aventi, the Ferrarese nobleman for whom Rossini composed *Ciro in Babilonia*; or in Naples, the Marchese di Berio, librettist of *Otello*, and the Duke of Ventignano, who gloried under the title 'the tragic poet of Naples', and wrote *Maometto II*. Jacopo Ferretti and Cesare Sterbini, Rossini's two Roman librettists, represent yet another class. Both were young men who earned their livings as

Jacopo Ferretti (1784–1852). Author of more than sixty librettos, four of which were also for Donizetti.

government employees: Ferretti, who was thirty-one in 1815, worked as director of the government salt-and-tobacco monopoly, and had a minor reputation as an Arcadian poet and later as a satirist. Finally there was Felice Romani, one of the few notable intellectual or literary figures who applied themselves to writing opera librettos, but who unfortunately only collaborated once with Rossini. A story told of Romani is a reminder of one aspect of the librettist's job which should not be overlooked and may explain why no figures of any literary eminence entered the field of opera, for the librettist was often expected, as far as we can tell, to supervise the staging of performances, a task which reduced Romani to despair when trying to get some semblance of acting out of Rubini during rehearsals for Bellini's *Il pirata*. It would have been enough to keep any really serious writer away from writing librettos.

We have a better documented account of the chronology of creation of *The Barber* than for most Rossini operas. Effectively, it was planned, written, learned, rehearsed and staged within the space of twenty four days. *The Barber* is not in this respect exceptional: Rossini claimed to have written *L'Italiana* in eighteen days, and *La Cenerentola*, which he began on December 25, 1815, was first performed exactly a month later on January 25, 1816. Rossini once said that he considered the forty days he was given to write one of his longest operas, *Semiramide*, a luxury, and completed it in thirty-three. Rossini's facility and fluency as a composer were famous, and illustrative stories such as that about the 'aria del riso' are numerous. But all composers of that period were under pressure to compose at speed; when Donizetti was told how long Rossini had taken in composing *The Barber* he is said to have replied: 'Ah, but then he always was a slow composer.' Rossini, Bellini, Donizetti, and for much of his life Verdi worked within a system which was frankly commercial, and in which they depended on selling their art in an open market like any other commodity; if the market demanded a great many operas within a short space of time, then Rossini and his fellow composers had to satisfy the demand or perish. In Italy at least, the era of protective patronage was over for the composer, and early nineteenth-century opera provides a perfect example of the extension of bourgeois economic principles to the field of art. The Italian composers could not afford to be torn by the conflicts that romantic artists elsewhere felt between expressing their creative individualism, and yet somehow having to sell the results, or products, to a generally unappreciative bourgeoisie. In the case of composers like Weber and Berlioz this conflict led to poverty, frustration, and eventually bitterness; in the case of Wagner, to the search for an eighteenth-century type patron who would allow him a nineteenth-century artist's licence, whom he finally located in Ludwig II of Bavaria. Rossini suffered no such agonising; he was a born conformer, and settled into the system as he found it. Mendelssohn, thinking of Donizetti, wrote: 'Northerners like work for its own sake, southerners because it brings money.' Mendelssohn meant this derogatively, but Rossini never felt any qualms about using his talents to earn money; and anyway, Mendelssohn was fortunate in being rich enough not to have to earn a living from his composing.

The Barber offers many examples of Rossini's habitual self-borrowing, a practice which he continued throughout his career. An attempt to list his borrowings would provide someone with a lifetime's thesis, and no doubt someone is at work on it at this very moment. They will discover that a duet from *Demetrio e Polibio* makes an appearance in five later operas, for example, and it does not take much scholarship to find out that the overture to *The Barber*, as we know it today (there is a suggestion that Rossini originally wrote a different overture which subsequently got lost), first saw the light of day as the overture to *Aureliano in Palmira*, was revamped with suitably martial additions for *Elisabetta*, and finally came to rest, shorn of its martial accretions, as the overture to *The Barber*, 'in which Rossini distils all the wit and spirit of his most famous masterpiece'.

Rossini was often accused of laziness by his contemporaries, scornful or jealous of the facility which allowed him so much leisure despite his enormous output, and his self-borrowing was often cited as evidence; but as Stendhal pointed out, a man who worked under such pressure as Rossini for most of his working life, and who had been so prolific, could hardly be called lazy; given the pressures under which he laboured, it is not surprising that he was forced to borrow. The practice was, and always had been, universal; when accused by an anonymous critic of the same sin, Donizetti wrote in reply: 'I do not know of anyone who does not make use of reminiscences, and if he wants to be kind enough to reveal himself, I will take him for a short stroll through the scores of someone whom he doesn't name and make him pick out from whichever of them he choses, not reminiscences, but whole pieces taken from I know not where . . .' Not until it became general practice to publish operas did composers have to be wary of repeating themselves, as Rossini himself realised to his horror when, in the 1850s, the publisher Ricordi planned to publish a complete edition of his operas. He wrote to Ricordi: 'I remain furious . . . about the publication, which will bring all my operas together before the eyes of the public. The same pieces will be found several times, for I thought I had the right to remove from my fiascos those pieces which seemed best, to rescue them from shipwreck by placing them in new works.' But in 1816 Rossini was safe: Ricordi had not published its first catalogue until 1814, and it took some years before it was publishing as quickly and universally as it was to in Verdi's day.

In many cases, Rossini's borrowings may have been subconscious, although this does not spare him the criticism that his music can all too often sound the same from one opera to the next, regardless of whether he were writing *opera seria* or *opera buffa*. As Spohr wrote: 'One is accustomed to hearing the same person singing now tragically, now comically, to hear from a peasant girl the same pompous ornamentation as one has just heard from a queen or heroine . . .'. This criticism is certainly fair, for it is undoubtedly true that, although more of his career was devoted to writing *opera seria*, Rossini's style was more naturally suited to comic opera, and it is for this reason that the music of the serious operas can all too often sound like that of the comic operas, and that his comic operas have survived where the serious ones have not. Years later, Rossini told Wagner that he was always much happier writing comedies, but that he had had little choice in the subjects of his librettos, which were forced upon him by theatre managers. And in Rossini's defence it can be said that one of his achievements in the historical development of opera was precisely the way in which he broke down some of the more rigid and antiquated conventions of *opera seria* by applying characteristics of *opera buffa* to *opera seria*, rendering the latter more flexible, and its characters more human.

Rossini's contract for *The Barber* is remarkable only in that it survives, but it offers some good examples of contemporary operatic practice. Rossini agrees to accept whatever libretto is given him, new or old (which bears out his complaint to Wagner), and to adapt his music to the voices of the singers. Rossini is to

Rossini's contract for *Il barbiere*.

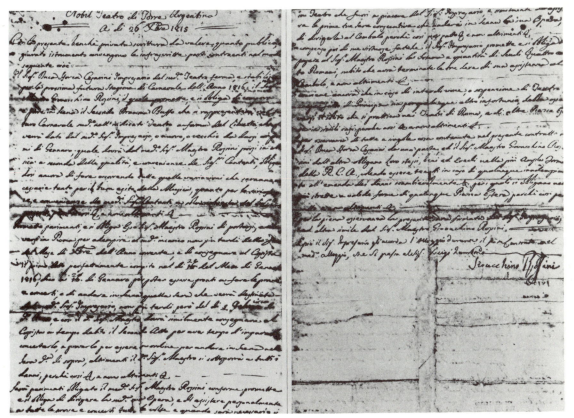

supervise the preparation of the opera, and is to conduct the first three performances from the harpsichord, a standard stipulation at this period; even long after composers had ceased to write *recitativo secco* (so that no keyboard instrument was necessary in the orchestra) they were apparently to be found sitting in the orchestra turning the pages for orchestral players for the first three performances of an opera. Finally, Rossini was to be paid 400 scudi; the *prima donna*, Righetti-Giorgi, was paid 500 scudi, for even at this date, when Rossini was one of the most famous composers in Italy, he was paid less than a *prima donna*, although it is true that the Roman theatres were famous for offering large fees to singers, a custom which Ferretti satirised when he wrote in 1834: 'Soon a city will be the price offered for a cavatina, and for a rondo an entire province.'

Perhaps the only surprise is that the contract does not stipulate a storm sequence, a feature that occurs in many Rossini operas from *Ciro* onwards, and of which he made something of a speciality.

7

Consolidation and development

On February 29, 1816 Rossini signed a contract in Rome for the following San Stefano season at the Teatro Valle, and then went back to Naples to fulfil his agreement with the San Carlo.

He returned to find the San Carlo a burnt-out ruin; it had been destroyed by fire on the night of February 12–13, and was already being rebuilt so as to be open in time for the following season in 1817. Meanwhile, the company was performing at the much smaller Teatro del Fondo, and here, in April, a marriage cantata was performed to celebrate the wedding of King Ferdinand's grand-daughter to the ill-fated Duc de Berry, son of the future Charles X of France.

In September, Rossini's second new opera for Naples opened at the Teatro dei Fiorentini, described by Stendhal as: 'A tiny theatre in the form of an elongated horseshoe, ideal for music.' The new work was an *opera buffa* called *La gazzetta*, and was based on a Goldoni play; it conformed to regional practice in that it was sung in local dialect. This was followed by a new *opera seria*, *Otello*.

Rossini's *Otello* has, of course, suffered comparison with Verdi's far greater version; but it was in comparison with Shakespeare that Rossini suffered at the time, especially since *Otello* appeared at a time when European Romanticism was just beginning to rediscover and appreciate Shakespeare. Byron, who heard that the opera was to be performed in Venice in 1818 was appalled, and wrote to Samuel Rogers in England: 'They have been crucifying *Othello* into an opera.' Then after seeing a performance, he recorded in his journal: 'The music good, but lugubrious,' (perhaps he should have been grateful, given Rossini's usual style) 'but as for the words, all the real scenes with Iago cut out, and the greatest nonsense inserted; the handkerchief turned into a billet-doux, and the first singer would not *black* his face, for some exquisite reason assigned in the preface'. Even Stendhal was disappointed; he rightly observed that Rossini was: 'Insufficiently master of his own idiom to describe such things.'

Both Byron and Stendhal were agreed that it was the unfortunate librettist who should take most of the blame, and this was none other than the Marchese di Berio, the famous Neapolitan man of letters and literary host who was said to know by heart much of Homer, Sophocles, Terence, Corneille, Alfieri and Shakespeare. But despite his great knowledge of literature, he was according to Stendhal, 'a man who is as charming a companion in society as he is unfortunate and abominable as a poet'. Yet it is

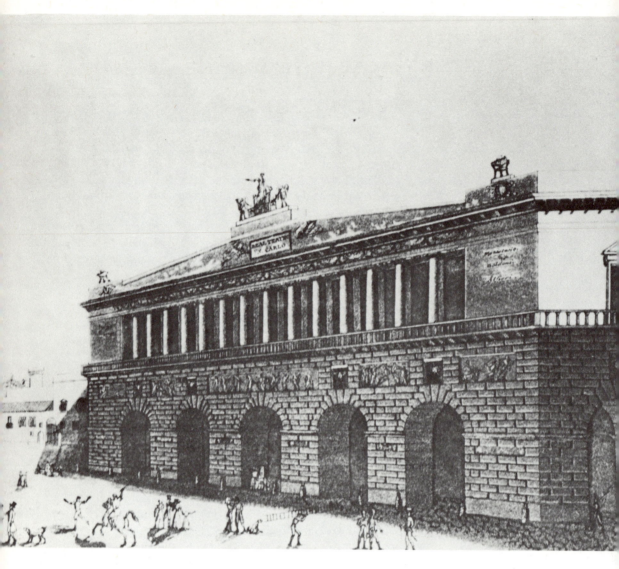

The San Carlo being rebuilt in 1816. The architect of the fine neo-classical façade of the theatre shown here was Antonio Niccolini.

unfair to condemn Berio too soundly for his adaptation of Shakespeare; Italy, like France, had always adhered to the neo-classical tradition in its drama, and knowledge and understanding of Shakespeare was still in its infancy. During the eighteenth century, Shakespeare's plays were only known in Italy through the heavily adapted French versions of Jean-François Ducis, and by 1816, only three of his plays had been translated directly into Italian: *Coriolanus*, *Othello*, and *Macbeth*. The first full edition did not appear until 1819–1822. We should also remember that even at this date scant respect was paid to Shakespeare in his own country, where in 1818 the 'adaptations' of Thomas Bowdler appeared, providing the language with a useful word for such efforts, 'bowdlerisation'.

Berio's own bowdlerisms are serious, but usually demanded by the conventions of Italian *opera seria*. Tradition demanded that the

Giovanni Davide (1790–1864). Son of the tenor Giacomo Davide, he was described by Stendhal as the greatest tenor of his age. He created the title role in Rossini's *Otello*, and the main tenor roles in *La donna del lago*, *Ermione* and *Zelmira*.

A brigand on the watch. A romanticised view by the French painter Leopold Robert. 1825.

hero be given a strong entrance aria, which Rossini and Berio consequently provide; but is this really so far removed from the spirit of the first appearance of Othello in Shakespeare, or so different from the spirit of the heroic entrance of Boito's and Verdi's Otello? In the last act, Berio and Rossini stuck very close to Shakespeare, and despite the convention that *opera seria* should not have a sad ending, retained the tragic close, which at later performances was often replaced, for fear of causing offence, by a happy ending (as when Giovanni Davide sung the role of Otello in Venice in 1822, and substituted the closing duet from *Armida* for Rossini's ending). Indeed, the final act of this *Otello*, with Desdemona's beautiful harp-accompanied willow song, and her moving prayer, is very fine, and quite worthy of Shakespeare. Meyerbeer, who must have attended one of the same series of performances in Venice as Byron, called this third act: '. . . really godlike. First-rate declamation, ever-impassioned recitative, mysterious accompaniment full of local colour, and particularly, the style of the old-time romances at its highest perfection.'

After the opening of *Otello* on December 4, Rossini set off back to Rome for the work he had contracted to write the previous season. This incessant travelling to and fro between Naples and Rome cannot have been pleasant, especially for a man of Rossini's hypersensitive temperament. No travel at this time was comfortable: the normal means was either by vetturino, a small hired coach which could be so slow that when Keats and Severn made the journey from Naples to Rome in 1820, Severn walked most of the way alongside the vetturino, or by post, when the traveller might expect to travel at about five to six miles an hour, and possibly, with ten hours on the road, fifty to sixty miles a day. The journey between Naples and Rome is over a hundred miles.

There were further inconveniences, for as the reader of *The Charterhouse of Parma* will remember, bureaucracy and officialdom are not twentieth-century inventions. The traveller who wanted to leave Naples had to secure about six different passes, and could expect to be stopped every few miles for custom checks. The journey was unpleasant in other ways; tourists observed with fascinated horror the numerous gibbets along the route with the bodies or limbs of executed criminals displayed on them. It was also dangerous; the poverty of the Neapolitan and Papal states meant that bandits were rife in the countryside. In 1812, Giovanni Colbran, the unfortunate husband of Isabella, wrote to the publisher Giovanni Ricordi in Milan that he and Isabella were unable to leave Naples 'because the road from here to Rome is full of bandits who are not satisfied with robbery, but also murder all who fall into their hands'. An English traveller, Henry Sass, journeying the same route between Naples and Rome in 1817 as Rossini in 1816, was horrified when he came upon 'a sight shocking to humanity, and disgraceful to the government in whose territory it occurred. Strewed in our path, and stretched in the arms of death, lay a traveller, the victim of assassination'. The journey was so dangerous that it was often impossible to get postillions to accompany the coaches, and the two governments were forced to post soldiers along the route. Even so, it was customary for voyagers to travel armed to the teeth with, as the Irish poet Tom Moore put it, 'pistols, daggers, sword-canes, etc.' This was travel on a main route between two major cities; off these routes it was a great deal worse.

It was supposedly on Rossini's journey to Rome in 1816 that Stendhal met him, at an inn in the village of Terracina, when Stendhal was on his way to Naples. The meeting is as fictitious as much else by Stendhal, for in fact he did not meet Rossini until two years later, in Milan; but as Lord Derwent writes: '*Se non e vero, e ben trovato*'. 'I noticed,' Stendhal recalls, 'among the seven or eight people a very handsome, blond man, a little bald, of thirty or thirty-two years [in fact he was twenty-four] . . . I told him that in my eyes, Rossini is the hope of the Italian school; I noticed that my man seemed slightly embarrassed; his travelling companions

Rossini. A portrait by Mayer, 1820. This is as Rossini must have appeared to Stendhal when he met him in Milan in 1818.

smiled; in short, it was Rossini himself.' As so often with Stendhal, his fictitious perceptions were far keener than most people's real observation. Rossini's slight embarrassment at Stendhal's praise is entirely characteristic. Unlike his younger contemporaries Donizetti and Bellini, Rossini was always sure enough of his abilities not to have to seek for praise or approbation: he seems to have possessed the serenity of self-confidence. But neither did he have an unduly inflated sense of his own importance. He knew he was no Mozart, and he was always ready generously to acknowledge the skills of other composers. These were the qualities that Stendhal recognised, and the qualities that made Rossini so attractive to his own contemporaries.

As was usual at this period, Rossini was lodged while preparing the new opera by the impresario of the Teatro Valle in the Palazzo Capranica, next door to the theatre—today the beautiful sixteenth-century palazzo is a cinema. It was probably a wise precaution, for it meant that Cartoni, the watchful impresario, could keep a close eye on Rossini who was inclined to alarm all impresarios by attending too many social functions and leaving the composition of whatever opera was in progress to the very last moment. When Spohr, who was in Rome at the time, tried to call on Rossini, he was turned away.

The gestatory problems of the new opera were hardly less traumatic than those of *The Barber*. The papal censor objected to the original libretto submitted (on political, religious, or moral grounds one wonders?) and Ferretti was called in. He, Cartoni and Rossini sat up late into the night chewing over suggestions and ideas. Ferretti recalled later:

I proposed twenty or thirty subjects for a melodrama, but one was envisaged as too serious for Rome then, at least during Carnival, when they wanted to laugh; this one was too complex; that one would have cost the impresario too much—and an impresario's views on economy must always be respected obediently by poets; and finally, another would not fit the virtuosos who had been designated.

Weary of making suggestions, and half falling asleep, in the middle of a yawn I murmured: "Cinderella?"

And so the opera was decided. Ferretti gave Rossini the first instalment of the libretto two days later, on Christmas Day. Rossini sprang into action, but seems to have found himself more than usually under pressure, and the opera was only just ready in time—and that with the help of another composer who had to be called in.

La Cenerentola is derived, as are all versions of the story, from a fairytale by the French seventeenth-century writer Perrault, via Felice Romani, who had conveniently made an operatic version for La Scala in 1814, adapting the story to the Italian *opera buffa* tradition. Ferretti's libretto is a plagiarism, but the morality of borrowing was different in those days, and the legal concept of copyright was not introduced until 1840. The first-night cast included Righetti-Giorgi, Rossini's first Rosina, but the performance was almost as much of a fiasco as that of *The Barber* a year earlier, an outcome which Ferretti attributed to 'all the bitter and untalented little maestri, and all the semi-redundant little maestri, who hated the new maestro to death, like pigmies at war with the sun'. Rossini seems to have had what was for him an unusually sure idea of the opera's worth, and predicted its eventual success. We should remember that, as one newspaper critic pointed out apropos of the first performance, by the first night of a new opera the performers must have been exhausted by the pressures of learning and staging a new work in an extremely short time, and that it would have taken three or four days for the singers to recover their full strength. It is therefore not surprising that so many first nights should have turned out as they did, and that operas were often ill-received at their initial performance.

On February 11, 1817 Rossini left Rome for Milan, where he was contracted to write a new opera for La Scala. On the way he stopped off at Bologna, where presumably he visited his parents, whom he had not seen for almost two years. Meanwhile in Milan, Stendhal, who was genuinely there, recorded in his journal: 'All Milan is in expectation of Rossini, who is to work on a libretto

La Gazza Ladra. Design by Sanquirico for the Trial Scene in Act II, the most impressive and moving scene in the opera, 1817.

Interior of the San Carlo.
The severity of the
exterior of the San Carlo
gives no indication of the
sumptuousness of its
interior.

entitled *La gazza ladra*.' The libretto for the new opera, which had originally been written for Paer who had then not used it, was based on a popular French boulevard play of a few years previously, itself based on a supposedly true story, called *La Pie voleuse*, ('The Thieving Magpie'). Its rustic setting and characters suggest a comedy, but its story is potentially tragic, hinging on a mistaken accusation against a servant girl for a theft committed by a magpie. It is in fact an *opera semi-seria*, that genre of which Stendhal so disapproved, and which led him to dismiss *La gazza ladra* as: 'The only too sordid horrors of that sordid little episode.' But *opera semi-seria* was important, for it allowed a composer to set a serious story using the more realistic vocal-conventions and less rigid formal structures of *opera buffa*. The libretto also offered Rossini an opportunity to provide a wider range of music than usual, with picturesquely coloured rustic episodes and cheerfully martial music for the military. Back in a city where he could expect a reasonably high standard of orchestral playing, Rossini seems to have attempted a greater subtlety and scope in his orchestral writing, perhaps encouraged by the recent popularity of several German composers at La Scala. Yet it was the greater complexity and power of Rossini's orchestration which set the traditionalists against him; one young musician was so incensed by the introduction of military instruments and drums into the score that he threatened to kill him. But despite all this, the opera was an enormous success, and the audience's response was described by Stendhal as being greater than he had ever heard before.

In August 1817 Rossini was back in Naples. The San Carlo had been rebuilt in a miraculous eleven months, and was now awaiting a new opera from him. By all accounts the new opera house was magnificent, although there were the customary detractors who turned up their noses at it. Henry Sass, with typically English primness, wrote of the new theatre: 'It is said to be the largest and most magnificent in Europe. In my opinion it is tawdry. When we visit a theatre we go to enjoy the scene, and not the gilding and decoration of the audience part.' Lady Blessington had no such qualms, and was delighted by the gilded palm trees which supported the royal box, surmounted by a splendid crown, but Spohr noticed a different drawback to such magnificence when he attended a performance in the very new theatre in February 1817:

The house is too large. Although the singers Signora Colbran and Signori Nozzari, Benedetti, etc, have very large voices, only their highest and most stentorian tones could be heard. If the theatre was really so sonorous before the fire, the improvements sought in the new construction have not materialised. Rather the reverse. The authorities would be well advised to throw out the superfluous decoration, which is heavy and not in the best of taste, and try and regain some of the building's former virtues.

Stendhal, who true to form was not actually present at the occasion, described the opening of the new theatre in glowing colours, including the uncomfortable moment when the heat of the candles caused the still wet plaster to steam, creating a moment's panic in the audience, who thought that the theatre was on fire again. But Stendhal too came to the conclusion that the end result was banal, and attributed what he believed to be Rossini's increasingly over-inflated orchestral writing to the vast size of the theatre.

Rossini's new opera was based on one of the most popular of all seventeenth and eighteenth-century operatic subjects, the story of the sorceress Armida from Tasso's epic poem *Gerusaleme liberata*, a subject which was also set by Lully, Handel, Gluck, Salieri, Haydn, and curiously Dvořák. But even in 1817 it was a thoroughly old-fashioned type of opera. The plot has a good deal of supernatural goings on, something which Rossini seems to have objected to, although whether from disdain, as a letter of 1835 would suggest, or because he was himself superstitious is not clear. Italians were famous for their superstition, and in particular, their belief that some people carried the evil eye; Heine teased Bellini mercilessly in Paris by pretending to be a '*jettatore*', or one who had the evil eye, and even the early twentieth-century philosopher Croce, a Neapolitan by birth, when asked about the phenomenon replied: 'I don't believe in it, but it's better not to joke about it.' Rossini almost certainly believed, and while setting the libretto for *Maometto II*, was said to have made the horned finger sign, which warns off the evil eye, against its author the

Duke of Ventignano, who was a famous *jettatore*. So very probably Rossini disliked setting *Armida* because he was himself superstitious.

Armida opened at the San Carlo on November 11, 1817, and was not a success, although not because it was too old fashioned, but because it was considered too modern musically. Rossini then trod the well-worn route up to Rome for an opera which opened at the Teatro Argentina on December 27, *Adelaida di Borgogna*. It is described by Radiciotti as the worst of Rossini's *opera serie*, and by Toye as 'an extremely tiresome mediaeval melodrama'. It was in part composed by his friend and crony of later years, Michele Carafa, Prince of Colobrano. Rossini returned to Naples and plunged straight back into work on a new piece for Lent. Relieved of the lugubrious Schmidt, the regular librettist whom Rossini found so gloomy that he had begged Barbaja to spare him interviews with 'this distressing person', he found himself landed with Barbaja's other tame librettist Andrea Leone Tottola. The result was *Mosè in Egitto* ('Moses in Egypt'), a biblical subject to suit the season, which opened at the San Carlo on March 5, 1818.

Mosè had to surmount two obstacles. Firstly, Rossini had returned to Naples to find that, because of his association with Colbran, he was at the centre of a political row. The situation in Naples was tense due to the split in governmental circles between the Ultras, or supporters of the principles of absolute monarchy, and the Liberals. Since the King was an enthusiastic supporter of Colbran, and hence of Rossini, there was nothing for the Liberals to do but set up an opposition claque at the San Carlo. The politics of Naples were being played out in the opera house, where one suspects the Italians would always prefer to play politics. Stendhal wrote: 'The theatre itself, and even Rossini, have become matters of party politics,' and discussing the crisis of a few years later, he wrote: 'In 1820 one thing alone would have made the Neapolitans happy; not the gift of a Spanish Constitution, but the elimination of Signora Colbran.'

The Liberals put up an opera called *Laodicea* by Morlacchi, at the time resident at the Italian opera in Dresden, and in the middle of a feud with Weber, who was trying to establish German opera there. The anti-Rossinians compared 'the old-time simplicity and nobility' of Morlacchi's music to the 'vain and false ornaments' of Rossini's, and the field was prepared for battle.

The performances of *Mosè* had more immediate problems to face than anything that Morlacchi could muster. The story of Moses and the Israelites fleeing Egypt presents technical problems which anyone without the resources of twentieth-century Hollywood would do well to avoid; not only plagues, but the parting of the Red Sea have to be presented. It was in this latter scene that the scenic department of the San Carlo came unstuck. Stendhal describes the scene:

In the third act the poet Tottola had brought in the Passage of the Red

Moses by Michelangelo. The appearance of Benedetti as Moses in the first performances was said to have been based on Michelangelo's sculpture.

79

Sea without considering that the Passage was not so easy to stage as the plague of darkness [seen in the first act]. Because of the way the parterre [or stalls] is situated, one cannot in any theatre perceive the sea except as from afar; here, because it had to be passed through, it necessarily had to be raised level. The San Carlo machinist, wanting to solve an insoluble problem, had done ridiculously incredible things. The parterre saw the sea raised from five to six feet above its shores; the loges [or boxes], gazing down on the waves, clearly perceived the little lazzaroni who made them open at the voice of Moses.

But despite the hilarity that the scene not surprisingly produced, it could not kill the overall success of the opera, which also allowed Rossini to triumph over his political rivals. The following year he inserted for a revival of the opera what has become the best-known number from it, the famous 'Prayer', which was intended to distract the audience's attention during the difficult moment of the parting of the waves. Its success was greater than can have been calculated; it was thought so powerful that a Neapolitan doctor attributed to it a number of convulsions and seizures amongst members of the audience, a complaint similar to that suffered by audiences stricken with '*Freischützfieber*' whilst attending performances of Weber's opera. But the prayer served its original purpose too; when Lady Morgan attended a performance of *Mosè* a few years later, she described the closing scenes in glowing terms that suggest that the scenic problem had been solved:

Moses gives the word to march, and moves his wand—the sea opens, and he leads his followers over the dry sands, amidst the plaudits of the audience, who retire from this fine opera vociferating through the streets 'Mi manca la voce'.

Even so, the parting of the Red Sea continued to cause problems to whoever else tried to mount the opera. When *Moïse*, the revised French version, was staged in Paris in 1827, the Red Sea scene which had cost 45,000 francs, had to be scrapped after the first night.

In the summer of 1818 Rossini went to Pesaro, his birth-town, which had planned to mount a production of *La gazza ladra* in its newly restored theatre. Rossini had helped with the arrangements from Naples, and played an active part in chosing the singers and orchestral players, whom he recruited from Ravenna. The opening of the theatre took place in June, and Rossini was the guest of a local amateur literary figure the Conte Pertacini, whose wife was the daughter of the famous poet Vincenzo Monti. The painstaking care that Rossini took over all the details of the performance shows a degree of artistic integrity in him that some might find surprising; he is even said to have concerned himself with the mechanics which operated the magpie itself.

Whilst in Pesaro, Rossini fell dangerously ill, and in Milan was reported dead; however, by August he was in Bologna, where he received a commission for an opera, *Adina*, to be performed in Lisbon. In September the official Naples Giornale announced Rossini's return to the city, and on December 3 a new opera, *Ricciardo e Zoraide*, with another libretto by Berio, was performed at the San Carlo. Although it has not survived in the theatre, it was a popular success at the time. At the beginning of 1819 Rossini was busy revising *Mosè* for the Lent season, writing a Cantata to celebrate the return of the King to good health, and preparing two new operas. The first, with a libretto by Tottola, was called *Ermione*, and opened on March 27. *Ermione* is another opera that has not stood the test of time; but there are few operas by Rossini which are without some fine music or some imaginative or innovatory dramatic stroke. This was especially the case with the operas Rossini wrote for Naples, where he was freer to develop his own musical and dramatic instincts. Several of these operas dispense with the customary overture, and in *Ermione* an offstage chorus is introduced into the prelude. *Mosè* is remarkable in that it contains the first major role written for a bass in Italian *opera seria*—basses were otherwise confined to minor roles and *opera buffa*. Gradually, Rossini was preparing the field for the full flowering of Italian romantic opera which was to follow.

Only a month after *Ermione*, on April 24, 1819, a new opera called *Edoardo e Cristina* was staged at the San Benedetto in Venice. Even for Rossini this was an impossible feat of speed, and in fact, the opera was not so new. It had been cobbled together from previous operas, with only seven out of the twenty-six numbers newly composed. The Venetian audiences, unaware of the deception, were delighted, amongst them Byron, whose affair with Teresa Guiccoli was to be conducted in large part at the San Benedetto the following year.

On his way back to Naples, Rossini stopped off in Pesaro. It was an unfortunate visit. Living in Pesaro at this time was Caroline of Brunswick, the wife of the Prince Regent of England. The marriage had been arranged by George III, and was a disaster; Caroline left England in 1814, and set off on a tour of Italy, providing a great source of embarrassment both to the English government and to her hosts wherever she went. In Milan she picked up a shady adventurer called Bartolomeo Bergami (or Pergami), who became her 'chamberlain' and lover, and the couple settled for a while in Pesaro. They were not popular in the town, and Rossini's friend Pertacini seems to have had a particular dislike for them; probably at his instigation, Rossini had refused to attend when invited to one of Caroline's soirées in 1818. The snub was not forgotten, and now on the 1819 visit, Bergami ensured that Rossini received an unpleasant reception. A special gala organised in his honour had to be scrapped by the authorities due to the threat of Bergami's hired thugs, and the local Accademia had to be content with installing a bust of the composer. Much to everyone's relief, Caroline returned to England in 1820.

Caroline of Brunswick, by Thomas Lawrence, 1804. In 1820, Caroline returned to England to claim her place as consort to George IV, and found herself tried for adultery instead. Acquitted, she died the following year.

In June, Rossini was back in what was now effectively his home, Naples. He had a new opera to write for September, and it was on an unequivocably romantic subject, drawn from Scott's poem of 1810 *The Lady of the Lake*. By 1819, Walter Scott was probably the best-known and most popular writer in Europe, and his picture of Scotland as the quintessentially romantic country was to capture the imagination of a whole generation. *La donna del lago*, with a libretto by Tottola, was the first opera to be written outside England on a subject from Scott. Rossini seems to have been moved by the romantic story to write music suffused with a certain lyric beauty that, with its picturesque setting, must have stirred many a romantic imagination. Stendhal describes the décor of the opening scene as showing 'a wild and lonely loch in the highlands of Scotland', which conjured up the 'magic of some Ossianic adventure'. The title role was sung by Colbran, who was first seen floating on the lake in a boat, and who, according to Stendhal,

Walter Scott (1771–1832) by Edwin Landseer, 1824. Scott's historical novels the first of which, *Waverley*, was published in 1814, were read all over Europe, and were extremely influential in the popular development of Romanticism. Over sixty operas have been based on works by Scott.

displayed 'considerable skill at the tiller of her skiff'. The first night audience did not respond favourably, and because there was no royalty present, were not inhibited by the etiquette that forbade anyone but the King to show approval or disapproval from letting their response be known. However, it was not long before it became one of Rossini's most popular operas, and even Leopardi, the greatest of nineteenth-century Italian poets and a near contemporary of Rossini's, was forced to admit: 'This music, executed by astonishing voices, is a stupendous affair, and even I could be moved to tears by it, if the gift of tears had not been removed from me.'

La donna del lago was followed by the long journey back to Milan for a new opera at La Scala. Rossini might have spared himself the trouble. Performed on December 26, *Bianca e Faliero*, was quite clearly run up in haste, and Rossini returned to the long abandoned practice in his *opere serie* of using *recitativo secco*, a device which certainly saved time. Who can blame him? La Scala was prepared to pay him 2,500 lire; *Bianca e Faliero* was the thirtieth of his operas, all of which, excluding *Demetrio e Polibio*, had been written within the space of nine years. Rossini was not yet twenty-eight, and had he died that year his fame would have been as assured as is the fame of Mozart who died at thirty-six, or Schubert who died at thirty-two. Furthermore, Rossini was no artist writing in the seclusion of an ivory tower; he not only wrote these operas, but was also responsible for their realisation on stage as well as preparing a great many other operas by other composers.

Above all, we should remember the incessant travel; the weary slog along dusty and dangerous roads in hot and uncomfortable coaches; the packing and unpacking of bags, the endless formalities at every state frontier, every toll-gate and every inn; the insalubrious inns themselves at which the traveller was forced to rest. It was, as Rossini later said to Wagner, 'the life of a nomad, to earn a living for my father, mother and grandmother'. Who will blame Rossini, if people were prepared to pay him money for giving less than his best? Stendhal recalled that Rossini was already talking about retiring when he reached the age of thirty.

8

Relaxation

What Verdi was to call 'the galley years' were over for Rossini. During the next four years he produced only four operas, which gave him a period of comparative rest before setting off on the different treadmill of international celebrity. By 1820 he was famous throughout Italy, and in February of that year a special festival, culminating in an 'Apotheosis of Rossini', was held in Genoa, a city for which he himself had never written an opera, or even visited.

In March 1820 Rossini was back in Naples, for in that month a Mass written in collaboration with Pietro Raimondi was performed in the newly built church of San Ferdinando. The Mass itself is a strikingly serious and fine work, but some indication of contemporary attitudes to spiritual music can be discerned from a description of the occasion left by a German writer who was present. It opened with an operatic overture by Mayr, followed by the overture to Rossini's own *La gazza ladra* (some years later Berlioz was taken aback to discover that Rossini overtures were commonly played on the organ in church services in Rome). The congregation—or perhaps one should call it the audience—applauded after the Gloria, 'as though they were in a theatre'; during the celebration of the Mass itself, 'the organ was played in a way that aroused pity. At the same time, the orchestra tuned up its instruments, while Rossini, in a loud voice so as to be heard, gave orders to this one and that one'. Even allowing for the disapproving tone of an over-serious German the occasion sounds bizarre.

The political situation in Naples at this time was fast moving towards a crisis. The previous year the Emperor Francis I of Austria had paid a visit to Italy, and had stayed with his father-in-law Ferdinand in Naples; Metternich had been in attendance, but although disappointed by the lukewarm reception the royal party received, he chose to ignore any signs of real discontent in the subject states. So did many others: the British minister in Naples described it as: 'A Kingdom in the highest degree flourishing and happy under the mildest of governments.' He could not have been more wrong; the Liberal minister Medici was fast losing ground to his more reactionary opponent Canosa, and in July 1820 the Carbonari, the revolutionary secret society, under General Gugliemo Pepe, marched on the nearby town of Avellino and captured it. The King was forced to accede to their demands for a Spanish style democratic constitution, and Naples was taken over by the new forces. It was a bloodless revolution, but it coincided

A patrol of Carbonari, Naples 1821. A contemporary lithograph.

with a rising in Piedmont in March 1821, which prompted Santorre di Santarosa, the leader of the Piedmont revolt, to declare that the events of 1820 and 1821 marked 'the first revolution in which two Italian peoples worked together at the two extremities of our peninsula'. Such nationalistic sentiments threatened the very principles of the Congress of Vienna, and Austria, Russia and Britain could not let them pass unnoticed. In December 1820, Ferdinand slipped off to Vienna to see what could be done about the worrying state of affairs in his kingdom.

In May 1820 Rossini had been given a new libretto by the Duke of Ventignano. When it was scheduled for performance we do not know, but the events of the summer threw normal activities into disarray; Barbaja was temporarily removed from his post at the San Carlo, and there was no theatrical activity in the city. Rossini, whom one is inclined to describe as craven when it came to

Paganini. A portrait drawing by Ingres, 1819. Ingres, an accomplished amateur violinist used to play second violin in a quartet in Rome with Paganini. Ingres' careful portrayal of the violinist is very different from the romantic image of the devilish violinist shown by Delacroix a few years later.

politics, went to ground. The opera, which eventually emerged in December 1820, was *Maometto II*, like *Tancredi* and *Semiramide* derived from the invaluable Voltaire, whose complete works had not yet been replaced by those of Scott and Hugo as the opera librettist's vade mecum. Weinstock suggests that stylistically *Maometto II* may owe something to the grand style of Spontini's *Fernand Cortez*, a revival of which in Naples Rossini had supervised earlier in the year, and this may have made it especially suitable for adaptation later as a French opera.

Maometto II was performed on December 3, 1820. By mid-December Rossini was back in Rome, where he was contracted to write an opera for the Teatro Apollo. Contrary to his usual practice, and probably due to the enforced leisure of the summer in Naples, Rossini had begun work on the opera before setting off for Rome. It had already been announced in Rome under the title *Mathilde*, but Rossini was dissatisfied with the still unfinished libretto, and turned to his old colleague Ferretti for help. Ferretti was too busy to recast the libretto or write a new one, but dug around and found an old one that he had previously adapted and gave it to Rossini. What had begun life as *Mathilde de Morwel* soon became *Matilda di Shabran*, an *opera semi-seria* with a quite different story, but the same music, and fortunately a heroine who shared the same name. Because of the last minute change and resultant rush, Rossini elicited help from the composer Pacini, an ardent admirer and imitator, who was later to inherit Rossini's position at the San Carlo.

Matilda di Shabran opened at the Apollo on February 24, 1821. The first performance was conducted by the great violin virtuoso Paganini, who took over when the scheduled leader of the orchestra had an apoplectic fit during the dress-rehearsal, and after a shaky start, it was well received. But despite the opera's success, the theatre's owner, Giovanni Torlonia, Duke of Bracciano, was not pleased. The Duke, who had taken over the management of the Apollo in 1820, was a member of the wealthy Torlonia banking family (bankers to Keats in Rome), and had more flair than some of his aristocratic colleagues as an impresario. He had set about reversing the appalling reputation of the Roman theatres, and had restored the Apollo, turning it into a popular social centre, with reception rooms, gambling tables and a café. Stendhal described it as 'the only decent theatre in all this great city'. Torlonia obviously considered it less important to engage expensive star singers for his theatre (the cast of *Matilda* contains no names of any renown) as long as he had a name like Rossini on his bills, therefore he was not very pleased when he found out that only half the new opera was actually by Rossini, and the rest by Pacini. He refused to pay Rossini the agreed fee of 500 scudi, and Rossini promptly went round to the theatre and collected up the score and orchestral parts, claiming that until he was paid they were legally his property. The performances could not continue, until an appeal to the Cardinal Governor of Rome resolved the matter. The opera ran until March 6.

The Duke's behaviour may have had some justification, since a description survives of the activities of Rossini and Paganini during the Rome Carnival that year, when Rossini should have been at work on the opera. During the weeks of the Carnival, the whole city was '*en fête*', and all normal restraints on behaviour were thrown to the wind. 'Love is no sin in Italy' wrote Lady Morgan wryly, observing the chaotic scene from the safety of a window. The festivities were opened every day by the firing of a cannon which marked the beginning of the famous wild horse race, the subject of some of the French painter Géricault's most powerful paintings. Then the crowds were free to take to the streets, and in all forms of disguise the population of the city paraded, danced and sang in the Corso, the main street that runs between the Capitol and the Piazza del Popolo. Amongst the throng that year were to be found Rossini and Paganini, who dressed themselves as women and took guitars with them, singing and playing in the crowd. The sounds of the Carnival must have reached John Keats, who lay mortally ill in his lodgings not far from the Piazza del Popolo. On February 23, a day before the opening of *Matilda di Shabran*, he died.

By the end of March, Rossini was in Naples again. His arrival must have coincided with that of the Austrians, for in January King Ferdinand had presented his case to the members of what was now the Quadruple Alliance, who were meeting at Laibach (present-day Ljubljana). The Austrians decided that it was their duty to intervene in Naples, and despite the protestations of the English, troops were sent to crush the revolt. Byron wrote gloomily from Verona in January: 'The Germans are on the Po,

The Roman Carnival of 1820. Engraving by Mörner.

the Barbarians at the gate, and their masters in council at Leybach (sic) . . . and lo they [the Italians] dance and sing and make merry.' And so, while the Italian peoples enjoyed the carnival season, the troops crossed Italy and arrived in Naples in March. King Ferdinand, who must be admired for his tenacious hold on his throne through so many vicissitudes if for nothing else, returned in April. The same month Rossini demonstrated his lasting affection for the music of Haydn by conducting a performance of *The Creation* at the San Carlo.

In December 1821 the horizons of Rossini's career were dramatically expanded. Barbaja, whose reputation was by now international, had been negotiating with the Kärntnertortheater in Vienna to take over its running and to bring an Italian company with him based on the Naples company. The brightest jewel in his crown was to be Rossini, and it was agreed that he too should go to Vienna. Rossini had already been casting his sights further afield; there had been a correspondence with the manager of the King's Theatre in London about the possibility of his going to London, and Hérold, in Italy in 1821 scouting for talent to bring to Paris, wrote home that Rossini was 'dying to come to Paris'. In January 1822, the official Naples Giornale announced Rossini's imminent trip to Vienna, Paris and London, his eventual return to Naples to be taken for granted.

It was decided that the new opera which Rossini was to write for Barbaja's company in Vienna should be given a sort of trial run at the San Carlo beforehand, and *Zelmira* opened there on February 16, 1822; the care with which the opera is written suggests that Rossini was concerned to write a piece worthy of the last home of Mozart and Haydn.

In February 1822, the same month as the opening of *Zelmira*, the twenty-five year old Gaetano Donizetti arrived in Naples; like Rossini, he had studied at the Liceo in Bologna under Padre Mattei, and also like Rossini, his first operas had been performed in Venice. In 1821 he arrived in Rome, and then hard on Rossini's heels made his way to Naples. On March 4 he wrote to his teacher, the opera composer Mayr, about a performance of Mayr's oratorio *Atalia* at the San Carlo, directed by Rossini. Donizetti was not impressed by the behaviour of the man who was only five years his senior: 'At the rehearsals, he complains Jesuitically about the singers, who don't follow him well, and then, at the orchestra rehearsals, there he is gossiping with the *prima-donna* instead of conducting.' It was accounts like this which gave Rossini his reputation for indolence and lack of seriousness, but one could just as well see it as evidence of Rossini's supreme musical facility—the sort of facility that easily led to envy in others less fortunately gifted.

Three days after this performance of *Atalia*, Rossini left Naples in the company of Colbran and several other members of the San Carlo company destined to join Barbaja in Vienna. Rossini and Colbran stopped off at her villa at Castenaso, near Bologna, and there, on March 16, they were married. Colbran had almost certainly been Barbaja's mistress at some stage, and had also been Rossini's, although for how long we do not know. But the transfer cannot have been too acrimonious, since Rossini and Barbaja always remained on excellent terms. As so often happens, the marriage seems to have been the beginning of the end for Rossini's and Colbran's relationship rather than a new start. Not only had Rossini married a woman seven years his senior, while he himself was still attractive and sexually active, but a partner whose career was virtually over. In December 1822 she had a palpable failure in a revival of *Maometto II* in Venice, and was whistled off the stage, and in 1824 she was described by Lord Mount Edgecumbe as 'entirely passée'. Inevitably, the marriage eventually broke down, and it is difficult not to feel that Rossini married Colbran for her money, for she was a wealthy woman, and owned large estates conveniently near Bologna.

9

Travels. Vienna and England

Biedermeier Vienna, the Vienna of Metternich, was also the Vienna of Beethoven and Schubert, the former at work on his Ninth Symphony in 1822. On March 27, Rossini attended a performance of Weber's *Der Freischütz*, conducted by the composer, at the Kärntnertortheater. But it was Rossini the Viennese were interested in, much to the annoyance of Weber, the disappointment of Schubert, struggling in vain to write an opera that might be accepted by a Viennese theatre, and Beethoven, still casting round for a subject lofty enough to inspire him to write a successor to *Fidelio*. The Viennese knew Rossini's operas well; they had already heard eight performed there, and now they were to have a four month season of nothing but Rossini, starting with *Zelmira*. In addition, they were to hear his operas performed for the first time by many of the finest Italian singers of that date, and by those for whom the operas had been written. In 1824, the philosopher Hegel described hearing Italian opera sung by Italians in Vienna for the first time as a 'revelation'.

Rossini's genius was unreservedly hailed by a city which had far greater geniuses in its midst. But Rossini appealed in some special way to the Viennese, who have always had a less serious, or earnest attitude to music than the Germans. Rossini was fêted and feasted; people fought to catch a glimpse of him, and paid for the privilege of shaking his hand; and with that peculiar display of adulation and greed so characteristic of an enthusiastic audience, demanded endless free entertainment of him. He was expected to perform at salons, at his hotel window, even in the street; nowhere was too inappropriate for yet another rendition of 'Largo al factotum'. Not until the arrival of Paganini in Vienna— when 'all classes of society came under his spell. Hats, gloves, boots, were all worn "à la Paganini". Walking-sticks and snuff-boxes bore the virtuoso's likeness. Even restauranteurs' dishes were named after him.'— was there a like reception for a visiting musical celebrity.

Rossini was far more interested in meeting Beethoven. He knew some of Beethoven's music, including the Third Symphony, the *Eroica*, which he had been able to hear while in Vienna, and wanted to meet the man who had composed it. Beethoven for his part was already well aware of Rossini's operas, having written a few years previously that, 'His music suits the frivolous and sensuous spirit of the age.' Beethoven was by now totally deaf, and had reached an extreme stage of antisocial behaviour, so introductions were difficult to secure. Rossini first tried an approach through the offices of the seventy-two year old Antonio

Vienna. The
Kärntnertortheater. A
print.

Salieri; Salieri, who had been Court composer in Vienna at the
time of Mozart, apparently in his old age had a passion for
composing canons, and used to come round to Rossini's rooms for
dessert after meals so that Colbran, Rossini, Davide and Nozzari
could sing his vocal quartets. Salieri was unable to engineer the
desired introduction, but Rossini persevered, and finally it was
arranged by the critic Carpani, one of the earliest biographers of
Haydn, and one of Vienna's most enthusiastic Rossini supporters.
The content of the meeting was described by Rossini years later, in
1860, at a no less remarkable meeting between the elderly Rossini
and Wagner, which was transcribed by Rossini's friend and
admirer Edmond Michotte. The authenticity of the account has
been questioned, but the only thing that need be doubted is the
memory of Rossini himself, recalling the meeting with Beethoven
almost forty years after the event; and the accuracy of Michotte,
who himself waited another forty years before publishing his
account. Otherwise, everything in the conversation rings entirely
true to what we know of the protagonists. The awe in which the
supposedly flippant and outwardly more successful composer held
the older man is perfectly apparent. Beethoven was
characteristically gruff, and his first words to Rossini were: 'Ah,
Rossini, you are the composer of *The Barber of Seville*? I

91

congratulate you, it is an excellent *opera buffa*; I read it with pleasure, and it delights me. It will be played as long as Italian opera exists. Never try to do anything but *opera buffa*.' It was pointed out that Rossini had actually composed a great many *opere serie*, which it transpired that Beethoven had looked through; but his advice remained the same. The meeting was short, for Beethoven easily tired of visitors; Rossini tried to get across his admiration (all communications had to be written down, so conversation was slow), but Beethoven's only reply was a sigh, and words 'Oh! un infelice.' His last words to Rossini were: 'Above all, write lots of *Barbers*.'

Schumann's description of the event captures its spirit movingly: 'The butterfly crossed the path of the eagle, but the latter turned aside in order not to crush it with the beating of its wings.' The great man's attempt, however gruff and graceless, to express his appreciation of Rossini's talents is indeed touching. No less so is Rossini's own attempt to get across his admiration. After the meeting, he was so appalled by Beethoven's apparent poverty that, at a gala dinner given by Metternich, he attempted to elicit some financial support for Beethoven from those present; but Beethoven's difficult behaviour and misanthropy were too well known for Rossini's effort to meet with much sympathy.

The fêting of Rossini culminated in a banquet held in his honour at which he was presented with a gift of 3,500 ducats. In July, he left Vienna for Bologna and Castenaso, where he and Isabella spent the remainder of the summer. Rossini bought a palazzo in the Strada Maggiore (now the Via Mazzini) in Bologna which suggests that he may have been thinking of settling in Bologna, probably so as to be near his parents. Otherwise, the summer was spent in writing some vocal exercises, *Gorgheggi e solfeggi*, designed to 'render the voice agile, and to learn to sing according to the modern taste'.

His peace was interrupted by a summons from Metternich for Rossini to supply music for the forthcoming meeting of the Quintuple Alliance, to be held in Verona. 'Since I was the *God of Harmony*,' Rossini later reported Metternich as having written, 'would I come there where harmony was so badly needed?'

Metternich was right; the triple alliance between Austria, Russia and Britain was shaky. Although the Tsar Alexander of Russia had abandoned some of his more liberal views, in accord with Metternich's desires, Britain was increasingly aloof, and at the 1822 Verona Congress, Wellington, who was attending because the British Foreign Minister Castlereagh had shot himself that summer, refused to commit Britain to intervention in Spain, which was undergoing a revolution. Rossini, for all his powers, could not bring harmony to such a tense gathering, but he produced all the necessary musical expressions for the desire for concord, and wrote the music for two 'spectacles', one of which was performed in the Roman arena at Verona, still a favourite setting for operatic performances. Rossini conducted, standing

Metternich (1773–1859). A portrait medallion on porcelain by Anton Schwindt, c1820. Metternich's complex system of balance of powers combined with extreme conservatism dominated European affairs between 1815 and 1848.

under a huge statue of Concordia which threatened to topple over and crush the performers. It managed not to, but concord *was* shattered when a dispute arose between Rossini and the authorities as to who owned the score and parts of the second piece, *Il vero omaggio*, for in a period before copyright laws, ownership of a score itself was what gave the right to perform a work. Rossini, who liked to plunder his occasional pieces for later operas could not afford to let the authorities in Verona keep the scores, and won his way.

In Verona, Rossini was entertained by the French poet Châteaubriand, who was there in his capacity as a diplomat and French representative; by Metternich, who was so keen an enthusiast for Rossini's music that he attended rehearsals of *Semiramide* in Venice the following year; by Tsar Alexander, the Emperor Francis of Austria, and Wellington. Rossini and Isabella then went on to Venice, where he was paid 5,000 francs to prepare a revival of *Maometto II* at La Fenice, ten times what he had been paid for his first commission at the theatre a decade earlier.

Semiramide. Design by Sanquirico for a production at La Scala in 1824.

Maometto II was performed on December 26, and on February 3 1823, *Semiramide*, his last Italian opera, opened at La Fenice. The librettist was his old collaborator Gaetano Rossi, and once again the story was derived from Voltaire, although the tale of Semiramide had also been one of the most popular of all Metastasian librettos. *Semiramide* marks the highpoint of the Rossinian *bel canto* style, a style to which he was never again to return. *Bel canto* means no more than fine singing, but fine singing of such a standard that the traditional training for a girl was five years, and for a man seven years. Rossini himself identified three elements which went to make *bel canto*: 1. The instrument—the voice; 2. Technique; 3. Style; the ingredients of which are taste and feeling. The object of such an exacting art was to produce voices which could cope with the widest and most taxing range of musical expression, and although highly florid and decorated music was not a necessary part of the *bel canto* style, it became generally associated with the meaning of the term, something that Rossini himself objected to. *Semiramide* contains some of Rossini's most demanding and difficult vocal writing, notably for the two principal female singers who play a mother and her son. Francis Toye describes the plot as a mixture of *Hamlet*, *Oedipus* and *The Oresteia*, and if the complications ensuing from such a mixture can be imagined (you have to imagine that Hamlet is also his mother's lover to get the full flavour) then it is a fair description.

Rossini and Isabella returned in March to Castenaso, where apart from writing a cantata in memory of Canova, who had died in Venice in 1822, they spent a tranquil summer. But Rossini was no Verdi; much as he enjoyed his leisure, he was essentially urban and cosmopolitan, and like so many of his contemporaries, a dandy. The life of a country gentleman did not suit him. All the same the future was in hand: Rossini was making the arrangements with Benelli, the new manager of the King's Theatre in London, for his trip to England. It is not surprising that Rossini should have been setting his sights further afield. The reception he had received in Vienna had given him a taste of the fruits of international celebrity, and an idea of the sort of reception he might expect elsewhere. London and Paris were richer than any Italian city (Mendelssohn wrote that in London and Paris 'one is better remunerated, more honoured, and lives more gaily at ease') and Rossini was certainly offered far more money for his projected London opera than he had been for his last Italian one. He also already had a great many English admirers who had come across him on their travels in Italy, and he arrived in England well furnished with letters of introduction from society figures such as the Duke of Devonshire.

And so, in October 1822, the Rossinis set out for London. They stopped off in Paris on the way, where Rossini immediately received a foretaste of the enthusiastic demand for him there, which eventually led him to make his home in the French capital. The attentions were by now familiar: bands that escorted him to his rooms, crowds that followed him in the street, and a huge banquet held in his honour at which the guests included the greatest French actors of the day, Talma and Mademoiselle Mars; the singers Giuditta Pasta and Rossini's old friend Manuel Garcia; the composers Auber, Boieldieu, and Hérold and the painter Horace Vernet. In his turn Rossini was expected to sing for his supper, and he was to be found in all the most glittering salons entertaining the rich, the idle and the bored with selections from his operas.

At some point during his stay in Paris, Rossini was approached by the Controller of the Royal Household, who was in charge of the Parisian theatres, with an offer for him to stay and work for the Théâtre-Italien. But he had his commitment in London to fulfil first, and so on December 7 he left Paris, arriving in London on December 13. Rossini and Isabella took rooms in Regent Street, and Rossini immediately took to his bed, shattered by the rough channel crossing. But news of his arrival soon got around, and messengers were sent from the King himself to enquire when Rossini would be well enough to present himself at Court.

The London that greeted Rossini in 1822 was the capital of a country far richer and far busier than his native Italy, and all the wealth, activity, intellect, and society was pooled in its capital. Although the former Prince Regent had lost his elegance and grace

Regent Street, showing the Quadrant (now destroyed). A print of 1822.

95

GIOACHINO ROSSINI.
MUSICAL COMPOSER, MEMBER OF THE FRENCH INSTITUTE.

ISABELLA COLBRAN ROS

Donna che per possente arte di canto
E per nobile azione maestosa
Mentre a ognuno di te formi un incanto
Vai fra le pari tue così famosa.

Non ti mancava, mi credio, che il v
Di poter di Rossin chiamarti spos
Egli ti scelse, caro aver ben puoi
Un tanto ammirator de' preg̀

Portraits of Rossini and Colbran published in 1824 in London in honour of their visit, with laudatory verses in Italian.

(he was now the corpulent and gouty George IV), the city he did so much to transform had not done so. Nash's white stucco facades were still fresh and gleaming, stretching from Regent's Park, down Regent Street, where the Rossinis had their lodgings at number 90, to Carlton House and Nash's recently remodelled King's Theatre in the Haymarket, the home of the Italian Opera in London.

England was not a land without music, but during the eighteenth and nineteenth centuries looked to the Continent for its musicians and composers; unlike France, England had failed to maintain a native tradition of any real strength alongside the foreign influx. London had been the first city outside Italy to see *The Barber*, and by 1823, eleven of Rossini's operas had been seen there, including the mysteriously titled *Peter the Hermit*, an adaptation of *Mosè* to suit Protestant sensibilities. Rossini was welcomed with all the enthusiasm and generosity which only a famous foreign composer could inspire in London society, and was offered £1,000 by the King's Theatre to write a new opera (although it is worth noting that Colbran was paid £1,500 for her appearances). Equally profitable for Rossini were the public

96

appearances he made at salons and soirées, for which he soon learned that he could charge a standard fee of £50. Even with such a stiff fee, he was in such demand that on his own reckoning he made about sixty such appearances, earning him a total of £3,000. No doubt he was as agreeably surprised by the desire of the English to be seen to support the arts as was the exiled Italian poet Ugo Foscolo, living in London at the same time, who, when paid £100 for a lecture on Italian literature, 'gazed at the crowded audience, and pocketed the gold with amazement,' unaware that the attendance of at least half the audience was the 'result of a poor vanity of appearing to take interest in what they did not understand'. Even so, Rossini never reached the financial heights of the singer Angelica Catalani, who in 1807 had managed to net the sum of £21,700 from her official operatic and concert engagements in England.

Another lucrative source of income was the giving of private lessons, for which Rossini was greatly in demand and for which he commanded as much as £100 per lesson; his pupils included Lady Holland and the Duke of Wellington, although how much singing the Duke did during his lessons is doubtful. Spohr, whose visit to London in 1820 brought forth all sorts of justifiably scathing comments about English musical life, also found giving private lessons a profitable activity, but had this to say about it: 'It was rather uphill work, for most of my pupils had neither talent nor industry, and took lessons only in order to be able to say that they had been pupils of Spohr.' The same must certainly have been true of Rossini's pupils.

Rossini at Brighton. A French engraving entitled 'La soirée de Brighton' (sic) showing George IV and Rossini. Rossini was described by Lady Greville in 1824 as 'a fat sallow squab of a man.'

Apart from various concert appearances, of which two took place in Cambridge in July 1824, where he played the organ in Great St Mary's Church and sang duets and solos in the Senate House, the highlight of Rossini's stay was his visit to Brighton to meet the King. It was four days after Christmas 1823, and George was staying in his newly-built Royal Pavilion. Having been presented to the King, Rossini was requested to sing some arias from his operas: this he proceeded to do, singing Desdemona's aria from *Otello* in falsetto, which those present judged to be in bad taste. A description of the occasion was left by Henry Edward Fox, the son of Lord Holland, who found himself suddenly summoned to the Royal Pavilion. Rossini, it would seem, was too familiar:

His Majesty was not much pleased with his manner, which was careless and indifferent to all the civilities shown him. The King himself made a fool of himself by joining in the choruses and the Hallelujah anthem, stamping his foot and overpowering all with the loudness of his royal voice. His voice, a bass, is not good, and he does not sing so much from notes as from recollection. He is therefore as a musician very far from good.

Rossini could not have disgraced himself too much at this first meeting, for he met the King on further occasions, and even sang duets with him at the famous Thursday-morning musical matinées of Prince Leopold of Saxe-Coburg.

The one disappointment of the visit, as far as London was concerned, was that the promised opera never appeared. Rossini conducted eight of his operas during his stay, but never wrote a new one for the King's Theatre. The main problem seems to have been the chronic financial trouble into which Benelli had got himself, and which eventually led to his fleeing the country in debt to the tune of £25,000. Not only had he assembled one of the most expensive companies ever seen at the King's Theatre, but at a late stage had decided that he also needed Angelica Catalani, who had last been heard in London ten years earlier. Unfortunately, she demanded half the box-office takings, which led Benelli into yet further debt.

The new opera was repeatedly announced, and it is known that its proposed title was *La figlia dell'aria* ('The Daughter of the Air'). So much mystery has become attached to Rossini's missing 'London' operas that it has been overlooked that *La figlia dell'aria* is simply another title for *Semiramide*, for the legendary Semiramide was reared by doves, and after reigning as Queen of Babylon, returned to the air from whence she had come. *La figlia dell'aria* was almost certainly none other than *Semiramide*,

The King's Theatre in the Haymarket. The home of the Italian opera in London since 1710, and the scene of the premières of more than twenty-four of Handel's operas. The exterior was remodelled by Nash in 1820 as part of his grand design linking Regent's Park with Carlton House.

possibly revised or altered in some way. In any case, by May 1824 news had got around that no new opera had yet been written. Rossini had probably been stalling because of the financial difficulties of the theatre; indeed, in February he had signed an agreement with the French Royal Household committing him to return to Paris in July, and so clearly had no intention of staying in London after this date. However, it was not until June that it was publicly admitted that plans for a new opera had fallen through, and Benelli, not one to cut his losses, then commissioned another opera called *Ugo re d'Italia*, to be performed in January 1825. Rossini was to deposit whatever he had written by the time he left for Paris in a bank vault, and he would be paid for the rest when the opera was performed. In the event, Benelli went bankrupt, and 'all the contents of the Opera have been advertised for sale: interminable disputes and litigation, mismanagement and repeated losses seem again to threaten ruin to the unfortunate King's Theatre'. *Ugo* was never completed, and Rossini was never paid. How much of it was actually written is uncertain, but in 1830 he wrote to England requesting the return of the score and of the £400 bond he had had to leave with it. The money, it seems, was repaid; the score was last heard of being passed from one firm of London solicitors to another, and then disappeared for ever.

10

Paris. *Guillaume Tell*

Before leaving for England in December 1824, Rossini had been approached by the Minister for the French Royal Household in charge of the Royal Theatres in Paris asking him whether he would be interested in taking up a position. Rossini stated his terms, which included the huge sum of 40,000 francs per annum, and the negotiations went no further. However, when Rossini's enormous success in London became apparent, it became imperative that, if the French were to be sure of securing him for Paris, his terms should be agreed to, and in February 1824, a junior official of the Royal Household came across to London and the contract was signed at the French Embassy. It stipulated that Rossini would write one opera each for the Opéra and the Théâtre-Italien, in addition to supervising the revival of another of his works.

The demand for Rossini's presence in Paris had largely been stimulated by two writers. In the spring of 1824, Stendhal's *Life of Rossini* was published in Paris. As a biography it is almost worthless; as a source of much fascinating detail about social and operatic practice in Italy it is invaluable if unreliable; as an example of sustained polemical journalism, it is a work of genius. While writing it Stendhal was living in the same apartment block as the singer Giuditta Pasta, and was able to follow the goings on of Parisian operatic life from a close viewpoint. He came to the conclusion that opera in Paris was in the doldrums. One reason for this was its curious organisational structure. Both the Opéra, the official French opera company, whose real title was the rather grandiose 'Académie Royale de Musique', and the Théâtre-Italien, the company devoted to Italian opera in Paris, came under the jurisdiction of the Minister of the Royal Household, who delegated artistic, as opposed to administrative, responsibility to the Director of Fine Arts. The holder of this post throughout the Restoration period (1815–1830) was the Vicomte de la Rochefoucauld, one of the richest landowners in France, and a man who was really far more interested in breeding race-horses than in encouraging the arts. His ignorance and incompetence were notorious, and there were few significant people in the artistic world of the Restoration who failed to cross paths, if not swords with him. Berlioz cited an example of Rochefoucauld's proverbial ignorance when he told the story of how he had once suggested to Cherubini that he should try his hand at writing an opera—the same Cherubini who had written thirty operas and was revered by the likes of Beethoven. One of Rochefoucauld's most

The Salle Favart, burned down in 1838, which, with the Salle Ventadour and the Salle Feydeau was used by the Théâtre-Italien between 1815 and 1876.

Rossini. A caricature by Benjamin, c 1824. The Opéra is collapsing, and the people appeal to Rossini to save it.

memorable contributions to the artistic scene was his insistence on lengthening the skirts of the dancers at the Opéra, in the name of purity.

At the time of Rochefoucauld's removal from his post in 1830, his enemies claimed that the Opéra was 1,200,000 francs in debt. But the effect of his rule was not just a financial disaster; it was also artistically barren. One contemporary described the Opéra as 'dying of langour, sleeping on its subsidy. The Académie Royale de Musique has fallen into such discredit, its receipts have diminished so greatly, its shriekings are held in such horror by everyone, that its most zealous defenders have joined the party of opposition in order to augment the number of mockers'. And yet a succession of operas were churned out for performance there, for as Spohr pointed out, the Opéra paid well—'Indeed, if it were not so lucrative to write for the Paris theatre, composers would long since have given up in disgust. But since a successful opera means profits continuing over a lifetime, new works appear almost every day'. But ever since the premature retirement of Cherubini, who had seemingly abandoned writing operas for amateur botany and painting, and the departure in 1819 of Spontini to Berlin, few of those new works were of great worth.

At the Théâtre-Italien the picture was, if less disastrous, not heartening. It had been run since 1812 by Fernando Paer, although it had suffered an unfortunate interregnum when Angelica Catalani had taken over for a season in 1814. Paer was a moderately gifted composer, but he failed to attract the most exciting figures in Italian opera to Paris, which had always been

The Salle le Pelletier, home of the Paris Opéra after the building in the Rue Richelieu was destroyed in 1820 by order of the Archbishop of Paris after the death of the Duc de Berry there.

the aim of the Théâtre-Italien. Stendhal even accused him of deliberately ignoring Rossini's operas out of jealousy, which is not true, for by 1823 twelve of Rossini's operas had been mounted there.

This was the state of opera in Paris in 1824, and Stendhal's *Life of Rossini* is a thinly disguised argument for reform on two fronts. Firstly, he believed that the Parisian theatres should be taken out of state control and run commercially, as were most theatres and opera houses in Italy; when this did eventually happen after the 1830 revolution, and the Opéra was put in the hands of a private entrepreneur, as Stendhal predicted, French opera gained a new lease of life.

Stendhal's second argument was even simpler: Rossini, the greatest opera composer of the age, should be brought to Paris. This was an argument also put forward by the critic and amateur musician Castil-Blaze. Castil-Blaze, who was equally aware that opera in Paris was at a low ebb, had a more unorthodox solution, for he was more directly concerned with the revitalisation of French opera, rather than just opera in Paris. He believed that French opera needed the example of both Rossini and Weber, whom he considered to be the pre-eminent opera composers of the period, and to this end he set about systematically making arrangements of Weber's and Rossini's works to conform to French taste (a policy he later advocated for the symphonies of

Charles X in coronation robes, by Ingres. Painted in 1829 from sketches made by Ingres at the Coronation in 1825.

Giuditta Pasta (1798–1865). The enormous range of Pasta's voice, and her famously dramatic portrayals made her the most sought after soprano of the 1820s. A miniature by Luigi Bianchi.

Beethoven). He hired the Théâtre de l'Odéon in Paris, and in May 1824 mounted a French version of *The Barber of Seville* there; this was followed in December by a bowdlerised version of Weber's *Der Freischütz*, entitled *Robin des Bois*. It was an enormous success, running for 327 performances, and was an important contributory factor in the development of French Romanticism; Berlioz in his memoirs claimed to have attended 100 performances. Fortunately, Paris was spared any further of Castil-Blaze's well-intentioned versions of Rossini's operas by the arrival of Rossini himself.

The original discussions and contract had made no mention of Rossini's exact position at the Théâtre-Italien; whatever arrangements were made, it could not but happen that Paer would be thrown into the shade by the ebullient talent of the younger man, who arrived in Paris as a conquering hero. In the event, it was decided, to save loss of face for Paer, that Rossini should be co-director. Paer then took a back seat and let Rossini get on with the running of the company.

In September 1824, Rossini and Isabella returned to Bologna to settle their affairs in preparation for their stay in Paris, and then came back to Paris for Rossini to take up his post in December. While he was away, King Louis XVIII died, and his brother, the reactionary Comte d'Artois, succeeded as Charles X. One of Rossini's first duties at the Théâtre-Italien was to compose a suitable piece to celebrate the Coronation of the King. The work was called *Il viaggio a Reims* ('The Journey to Rheims') (Rheims was the traditional place where French monarchs were crowned), and contained the usual mixture of patriotic choruses, allegorical ballets, expressions of loyalty to the new monarch, and to make the evening complete, a pot-pourri of national anthems. Charles X himself attended the première on June 19, and was too obviously bored. It was an occasional piece, and not intended to outlive the occasion for which it was written, although Rossini, never one to waste effort unnecessarily, salvaged much of the music for his later *Le Comte Ory*. However, the cast assembled for *Il viaggio a Reims* is indicative of the beginnings of a shift to Paris as the centre of opera in Europe, a shift which Rossini was largely instrumental in bringing about. It included Giuditta Pasta, fast establishing herself as the greatest soprano of her age, having taken Paris by storm in 1822, the French soprano Laura Cinti-Damoreau, who was later to create the soprano roles in Rossini's four French operas, and the great French bass Nicolas-Prosper Levasseur.

Il viaggio was performed in June 1825, and Rossini's next undertaking was the first Paris production of Meyerbeer's last Italian opera *Il crociato in Egitto*, over which Rossini took immense pains. He introduced two further Italian singers with whom he had worked before, Ester Mombelli, and the tenor Domenico Donzelli, and in October he introduced the tenor Giovanni Battista Rubini, who was soon to become the finest tenor of the period, in *La donna del lago*; and then in December Rossini

Costume designs for the première of *Le Siège de Corinthe*, 1826.

produced *Semiramide*, and in March 1826, *Zelmira*. But where was the promised new opera? The Parisians were disappointed, and accusations of laziness began to be thrown at Rossini, not without justification, as John Ebers, the new director of the King's Theatre in London confirmed when he visited Rossini in Paris and reported that he was 'in great repute in Paris, and mixed a great deal in society, to which his social and happy temperament inclines him. He spent his time in agreeable union of the occupations of director and bon-vivant'. Even Stendhal felt prompted to enquire: 'May one be so bold as to ask this illustrious man what he has done up till now for the good Parisian public which is so fond of him?'

Rossini's contribution to Parisian society was not confined to displaying his verbal wit or musical facility in the various salons in which he was so much in demand. One of the popular causes to which much of Paris society currently subscribed was that of Greek liberation from the Turks, always readier, like all societies, to condemn ills abroad than those on their own doorstep. The Greek war of liberation had been going on since 1821, but had probably been brought to the attention of most people by the death of Byron in Missalonghi in April 1824, to commemorate which Rossini had written a cantata called *Il pianto delle Muse in morte di Lord Byron* ('The lament of the Muses for the death of Lord Byron'). In Paris charity concerts were held to help the Greek patriots, and one of these concerts, which raised 300,000 francs, was conducted by Rossini.

In June 1826 Rossini resigned his post at the Théâtre-Italien, obviously deciding that he no longer wanted to be involved in the routine responsibility of running such an institution. But the Royal Household had enough acumen to realise that Rossini should be kept in Paris, so in October 1826 a post was invented for Rossini in which he was designated Chief Composer to the King and Inspector General of Singing in France, with an annual stipend of 25,000 francs; Rossini relished the Gilbertian absurdity of the title, but the stipend was certainly no joke.

Finally, on October 9, 1826 Rossini's first French opera was staged, although it was in fact only a remodelling to suit French taste of *Maometto II*. It was called *Le Siège de Corinthe* ('The Siege of Corinth'), and capitalised on the fashionable struggle going on in Greece, its story based on an earlier historical conflict between Greeks and Turks, with a heroine who sacrifices herself for her country. *Le Siège* was the first opera for which Rossini sold the performing rights direct to a publisher, the wealthy amateur mathematician and music lover Eugène Troupenas.

The same month an opera called *Ivanhoé*, with music by Rossini, appeared at the Odéon. It was in fact what was known in those days as a '*pasticcio*', or pastiche, an opera cobbled together from music written for other operas. Rossini himself had no hand in it, and got no financial reward for it; hence his care in securing the score of a work like the Verona cantata. *Ivanhoé* was based on

Walter Scott's novel of the same name. Scott himself attended a performance and described the occasion:

In the evening at the Odéon, where we saw *Ivanhoe*. It was superbly got up . . . the number of attendants, and the skill with which they were moved and grouped on stage, were well worthy of notice. It was an opera, and of course the story greatly mangled, and the dialogue in great part nonsense.

Scott must have been well used to such things, since it was customary in London every time one of his novels appeared to stage a musical version, and one can be quite sure that the music would have been a great deal less distinguished than that which Scott heard at the Odéon.

In March 1827 Rossini's second French opera was staged at the Opéra, and again it was a refashioning of an earlier opera, this time his *Mosè*, whose title now became *Moïse et Pharaon, ou Le Passage de la Mer Rouge*. The biblical subject, which Rossini told Hérold he had made even more religious than any sacred text, and the lofty theme of the conflict between love and duty in a fashionably patriotic setting gave the opera an instant appeal. For French audiences Rossini had reduced the proportion of arias and considerably simplified the vocal writing, so that what had formerly been florid and ornate became more simply and powerfully expressive and consequently even the severe Cherubini, now Director of the Conservatoire and no lover of Rossini's music, had to admit his admiration. But for many people it was not the

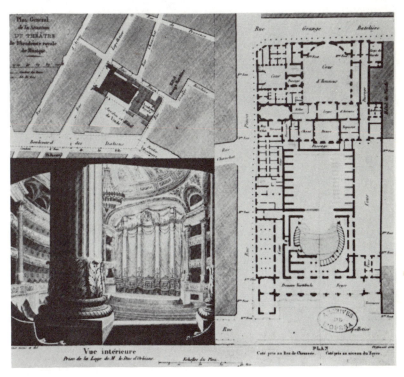

The Salle le Pelletier, showing a plan of the theatre, and a view of the interior as seen from the box of the Duc d'Orléans.

105

pruning of the florid vocal writing that was significant, but rather that Rossini had introduced pure Italian vocal lyricism into French opera, something that Cherubini and Spontini, with their adherence to the more severe, declamatory tradition established by Gluck, had never attempted. It was the first step towards *Guillaume Tell* and Meyerbeer.

Just before the opening night of the new opera, Rossini received news that his mother had died of a heart complaint at the age of fifty-five. Rossini, who like many Italians was devoted to his mother, was noticeably shattered, no doubt all the more so because his lifestyle had forced such long periods of separation from his parents. The family doctor in Bologna had forbidden Rossini to be called for when it was known that his mother was seriously ill, for fear that his return might shock her and her death be prematurely brought on; his previous visit had so excited her that she had been forced to stay in bed for two weeks, an indication of the emotionalism and hypersensitivity that was prevalent at this date.

Rossini's first reaction to his mother's death was to summon his father to Paris, where they could comfort each other. But it is also clear that he was already thinking of returning to Bologna, which he had come to think of as his home, and where the palazzo he had bought in 1822 was now being prepared for his eventual homecoming. Meanwhile, he continued to work at a leisurely pace. His social life followed the pattern of the rest of Paris; much of his time was spent staying in the villa of his friend and patron, the Spanish banker Alejandro Aguado, at Petit Bourg on the outskirts of Paris. In November Rossini and Isabella made a fashionable trip to the seaside at Dieppe. Not surprisingly, he found it bleak and dismal, no doubt furthering his resolve to return to the warmth and sun of his native country. Meanwhile, he was working on a French comic opera, his first original French opera. This was *Le Comte Ory*, which had a libretto by Eugène Scribe and Delestre-Poirson. Scribe was a prolific and hugely successful playwright, as well as an important and influential librettist, although with *Le Comte Ory* he did not exercise the strong creative influence over the composer that he was later to have over Auber, Halévy and Meyerbeer, the composers with whom he was most closely associated, for he was simply adapting an existing one-act vaudeville to Rossini's needs.

Those needs at the time were quite simple. He knew that a French grand opera was expected of him, and he almost certainly felt that before he was ready to tackle this he would try his strength on a slighter French work, and one in a vein in which he felt secure. Hence his setting a comic work, although *Le Comte Ory* is rather different from his earlier Italian comic operas. Although the *buffo* elements are clearly present, a number like the famous trio in Act II 'A la faveur de cette nuit obscure' has a sensuous suavity that made even Berlioz exclaim: 'What musical riches! A wealth of felicitous airs throughout, and finally, that wonderful trio,

Eugène Scribe (1791–1861). Scribe was in his own right an immensely successful and enormously prolific playwright, the greatest practitioner of the 'well-made-play'; but his opera libretti include thirty-eight for Auber alone, as well as that for *Le Comte Ory*.

Rossini's masterpiece in my opinion.' Another enthusiast for the opera was Liszt, who staged it at Weimar.

Le Comte Ory was performed on August 20, 1828 at the Opéra. After the first few performances, Rossini again retired to Aguado's villa at Petit Bourg, and perhaps given confidence by its success, set to work on the long promised serious French opera. The new work had been expected for some time. Castil-Blaze had written as long ago as 1825: 'We await his French grand opera,' and Rossini had delayed setting to work for long enough. The moment now seemed ripe. He had had four years in which to come to terms with the problems of setting French words, and had now had a trial run. Furthermore, standards in singing had improved at the Opéra while Rossini had been in Paris, giving an added incentive. The most important figure in this revival of French singing was the tenor Adolphe Nourrit. Nourrit was an intelligent and enterprising man in his own right, but as a singer made an important contribution to Parisian musical life. Contemporaries described him as an intensely serious and committed singer; 'He practised his profession as if it were sacred, and made of his art a

Le Comte Ory; a drawing showing Nourrit as the Count (left), and again disguised as the Hermit (right) with the page Isolier.

Adolphe Nourrit (1802–1839), as Arnold in *Guillaume Tell*. Nourrit appeared in the premières of *Le Siège de Corinthe* and *Moïse*, and is said to have helped Rossini with the setting of the French texts of these works.

kind of religion,' we are told; he 'carried his energies into the smallest details of a role, and from beginning to end lived the life of the character he was creating entirely.' Not content with concerning himself with his own contribution:

He cared for everything; studying his role, putting it together and recreating it were the least of his worries, for he had also to take charge of thousands of details concerning the staging of an opera, and lived through the other characters as if they were his own.

It was Nourrit who introduced the songs of Schubert to Paris, often singing them in his own translations; he also wrote the scenarios for several ballets, including that for the still popular *La Sylphide*.

In February 1828 Nourrit appeared in Auber's *La Muette de Portici* at the Opéra. Auber's opera has often been called the first French grand opera: with its epic historical setting, its stirring revolutionary subject, and its opportunities for picturesque local colour it certainly presages many of the operas which were to follow it on the stage of the Opéra. But what is more significant is that those are all qualities which apply even more specifically to Rossini's *Guillaume Tell*, and that the success of Auber's work must have pointed the direction for Rossini when he came to consider his own contribution to the genre of French opera. He first of all considered two librettos by Scribe, both of which later surfaced, one, *La Juive*, set by Halévy, and the other, *Gustave III ou Le Bal masqué*, set by Auber and later, adapted, by Verdi. But instead Rossini chose an adaptation of Schiller's epic play *Wilhelm Tell* by Etienne de Jouy, a playwright, and the librettist of Spontini's *La Vestale* and *Fernand Cortez*. Having reached Aguado's villa at Petit-Bourg, however, Rossini found that the libretto he had was far too cumbersome, and called for help in reworking it from Hippolyte Bis, and then from Aguado's secretary Armand Marrast, later a well-known liberal journalist, and Mayor of Paris and President of the National Assembly during the Second Republic.

The birth pangs of the new opera were followed as closely in the Paris press as the birth of a royal baby. On October 15 the opera was well under way; then it was reported that some of the music had been sent to the copyists. This was followed by a long pause, which gave rise to further anxious speculation, until rehearsals began in May 1829. The delay was due to a row between Rossini and the Royal Household over a new contract. He wanted a lifetime's annuity from the French government of 6,000 francs (remember, he was still only thirty-seven, and could expect another good twenty-five years of life ahead of him), in return for which he would give a vague undertaking to write five operas over the next ten years. The government baulked at this, and Rossini tried several ploys to win them round, pointing out that he had had 'much more advantageous conditions' offered him repeatedly by

England, Germany, Russia and Italy. Not content with this blatant manipulation of French vanity, Rossini threatened to withdraw the score of *Tell* unless his conditions were agreed to. Still no new contract was forthcoming, and so Rossini did as he had threatened, and withheld the music. The Director of the Opéra, Lubbert, in despair since everything else was ready and the dates fixed, appealed to the Royal Minister, and finally, on May 8, 1829, Charles X signed the new agreement. Everyone breathed a sigh of relief, and the rehearsals went ahead. It is not an attractive incident, and shows once again that Rossini possessed in full measure the unbeatable combination of ruthlessness and charm.

The première drew near, and the sense of expectation grew yet greater. Lady Morgan, who was in Paris at the time, wrote in her journal: 'For the last months of our residence in Paris, nothing has been talked of in the world of musical fashion, but the expected opera of *William Tell*.' Lady Morgan was unable to attend any performances, but instead went to an open dress-rehearsal. Rossini, relaxed and at ease, coaxed the musicians, aloud, "*caro violoncello too piano*", or "*signor mio flauto too forte*", in the gentlest voice and most supplicating tone.' If he was nervous about the forthcoming première, he did not show it.

The first performance, on August 3, 1829, was conducted by Habeneck, the founder and director of the Société des Concerts du

Guillaume Tell. A bill announcing the first performance on August 3, 1829.

Conservatoire, and the man responsible for introducing the symphonies of Beethoven to Paris. The new opera's great length precluded an instant response from the audience but the considered opinion of the Press and most subsequent writers was that this was Rossini's masterpiece, as indeed in some ways it is. Although in many respects the libretto is still cumbersome, despite the doctoring of Marrast, the opera has a nobility and seriousness which sets it apart even from works like *Moïse*. The epic scale of Schiller's play is more than matched by Rossini's music, especially in a scene like The Gathering of the Cantons, which has a sense of dramatic build-up and sweep rarely equalled in opera. The music is throughout of extraordinary richness and expansiveness, and is orchestrated with rare imagination and felicity, from the opening bars scored for mysterious solo cellos, to the true greatness of the final pages of the score, a hymn of liberty that rises with the sun over the Alps, and, to quote Berlioz, 'mounts to Heaven, calm and imposing, like the prayer of a just man'.

Although *Guillaume Tell* achieved 500 performances in Paris alone during Rossini's own lifetime, it underwent many vicissitudes that point to the musical taste of the time. Its immense length (over four hours of music) meant that not only did it suffer cuts, but that eventually only the popular second Act was performed at all, usually with excerpts from other operas. Once, when Rossini was told that the second act was to be performed at the Opéra, he replied 'What, all of it?' The practice of presenting excerpts did not shock Rossini's contemporaries as much as it shocks us, who tend to have a more reverential attitude towards works of art; in *I Capuletti ed i Montecchi*, Bellini's version of *Romeo and Juliet*, another version of the last act from an opera by Vaccai was often preferred and happily substituted. Often it was simply a matter of audiences enjoying a selection of popular favourites or 'bleeding chunks'; in 1847, Delacroix recorded in his journal that he had attended a performance at the Théâtre-Italien which consisted of the first Act of Cimarosa's *Il matrimonio segreto*, the second Act of Verdi's *Nabucco*, and the second and third Acts of Rossini's *Otello*. Single Acts of *Moïse* were often played as curtain raisers to an evening's opera.

11

The great renunciation.
Rossini and Romanticism

Guillaume Tell was Rossini's last opera. Inevitably, when an artist at the height of his powers ceases to create, speculation sets in as to why. The simple answer is often that he has no more to say, and one could wish that a few more creative artists with nothing left to say had had the honesty and integrity to admit it and give up. In Rossini's case it is not quite so straightforward, for Rossini did not, in the first place, write music because of a need for creative self-expression; he wrote music because it earned him a living. At a later date Wagner was to regret that Rossini had never been fired by the 'holiness' of his art. Exactly! As Stendhal said to Lady Morgan when she commented that Rossini's playing and singing were 'more like inspiration than mere human genius,' 'Inspiration! If you were to talk to him of inspiration, he would laugh at you'.

It is important to remember that, if Stendhal is correct, Rossini had already declared in 1819 that he intended to give up composing in two years time. That he did not do so may have been due to the break afforded him by his trip to Vienna, and his subsequent stays in London and Paris. In these cities, however, Rossini discovered that there were easier ways of making money than by writing operas, and if, in 1829, the French government was prepared to commit itself to paying him a lifetime's annuity for no more than a very vague undertaking on his part to spend a certain amount of time in Paris every year, well then, what need to continue writing operas? He had to fight for the annuity in the event, but it is still clear that by 1829 he had made enough money not to have to worry about writing new operas. When the need to earn a living had ceased, the need to compose ceased too.

Here is at least a part of the answer, even if it does mean taking a rather cynical attitude to Rossini as a creative artist. But, as we have seen, Rossini was nothing if not venal. Yet it is not the whole answer. Rossini did not cease to consider writing operas immediately after *Guillaume Tell*. In September 1829 Rossini and Isabella were back in Bologna, and in March 1830 he was having what turned out to be fruitless discussions with Edouard Robert, one of the new directors of the Théâtre-Italien, about a new opera. In May, Rossini wrote to Rochefoucauld that he was expecting a libretto to be sent to him, and complaining that it had not yet arrived. He was also at about the same time enquiring after the score for the unfinished opera that he had left in London. He later remembered that amongst the subjects he had considered were *Faust*, *Ivanhoe* and Joan of Arc.

Rossini in 1830. A portrait by L. Nauer.

The 28th of July. *Liberty leading the People* (often called *Liberty on the Barricades*). Delacroix, 1830. The workers and the bourgeoisie (the young man in a top hat), united against the forces of reaction, are being led to victory by the figure of Liberty.

And then in July 1830 Paris was shaken by revolution; the reactionary Charles X lost his throne and was replaced by the 'bourgeois monarch' Louis-Philippe. Paris was a long way from Bologna, but as usual, revolution in Paris was followed by unrest elsewhere in Europe. There were risings in Belgium (sparked off by a performance of Auber's *La Muette de Portici*), in Austria, and in central Italy, where Bologna itself was the centre of revolt; in 1831 a short-lived popular provisional government was set up there. Because the government of Louis-Philippe had espoused a policy of non-intervention abroad, the Austrians were able to crush the revolt with ease. But Italy had attained a new revolutionary consciousness, and in 1831 the twenty-six year old Mazzini, exiled from Italy for his republicanism, set up his headquarters in Marseilles and founded the 'Young Italians', an organisation dedicated to the expulsion of foreign rulers from

Giuseppe Mazzini (1805–1872) as Triumvir of Rome in 1849. Mazzini provided the intellectual stimulus for the Risorgimento, but lived most of his life in exile from Italy.

Giacomo Meyerbeer (1791–1864).

Italy, and the unification of all Italy under one republican flag. By 1833 the organisation had 60,000 members, and the Risorgimento had come into being.

It was the events of July 1830 and the months which followed that determined Rossini's decision to stop writing operas. In May Rossini is still talking about a new opera; two months later comes the July Revolution, and no more is ever heard about a new work. Why did the events of 1830 and '31 effect his decision to give up composing?

The most immediate way in which Rossini was affected by the revolution of July was through his association with the Paris Opéra. The revolution shattered the centralised system of French political control based on the crown, and opened doors to the dynamics of the new bourgeois system. As part of the old system, the Opéra found itself transformed along with everything else. Its administration was put into the hands of that curious figure Louis Veron. Veron, entrepreneur and charlatan, a figure who might have come from a novel by Balzac, determined to run the theatre along dynamic business lines, and introduced the principles of commerce into theatre management. His success lay in his ability to gauge the taste of his audiences for spectacular theatre, a taste which he supplied amply. Under the stage designer Ciceri the scenic department of the Opéra, hitherto said to be the 'most neglected branch of the Opéra', was transformed. The splendid visual spectacles at the Opéra soon became famous, and Nourrit, alarmed, wrote of Veron: 'Poetry, music, song and dance are only the pretext to set off his splendour'. But the pretext was nonetheless important, and it was part of Veron's achievement to develop the partnership of Scribe and Meyerbeer which provided such splendid vehicles for the required spectacles.

Meyerbeer, an exact contemporary of Rossini, was a German Jew, a fellow-pupil of Weber's in Vienna under the Abbé Vogl, who had then spent many years in Italy learning the rudiments of the Italian operatic style. His first Italian opera was written in 1817, and was followed by five further operatic works in imitation of Rossini. Eventually he followed Rossini to Paris, and here, in 1831, his *Robert le diable*, with a libretto by Scribe, was produced at the Opéra. In *Robert* Scribe and Meyerbeer were able to produce 'something for everyone', as Mendelssohn put it. It is full of popular romantic themes: mediaeval chivalry, Gothic horror, a demon recalling the one in *Der Freischütz*, a typical romantic hero, and a spicy combination of piety and blasphemy. Musically too it contains something for everyone: bold and exciting orchestral scoring, *bel canto* for the lovers of Italian opera, an offstage organ, and heavenly choirs. *Robert le diable* was one of the most popular operas of the whole nineteenth century, and for long set the standard for new operas in Paris.

To a certain extent, the success of *Robert* and of its creators displaced Rossini. This alone would not have been enough to determine his renunciation; it is certainly ironic that Meyerbeer, who was the same age as Rossini, and who had assiduously assimilated Rossini's style over the years, should have begun his true career at the moment that Rossini's finished. But this is a retrospective irony; there seems never to have been any resentment or bitterness on Rossini's part towards Meyerbeer for having superseded him. Rossini was always extremely generous in his dealings with other composers, and despite the many legends to the contrary, Meyerbeer and Rossini were always very fond of each other, and remained friends for the rest of their lives. When Meyerbeer died in 1864, Rossini was obviously upset, and wrote a brief musical tribute.

What is more ironic about the success of *Robert le diable* and the operas which followed it is that it was Rossini's own *Guillaume Tell* which had spawned the monster that became French grand opera. With its immense length, its huge choruses and tableau-like scenes, its historical setting, and its extremely demanding vocal

Robert le Diable (1831). The scene depicted on stage is the famous Ballet of the Nuns. The main role in the ballet was danced by Maria Taglioni.

writing, in particular for the tenor (whose part, according to an analysis by that fine amateur tenor James Joyce, contains nineteen top Cs and two C sharps), *Guillaume Tell* is, as Wagner observed, the prototype grand opera. The truth is that Rossini realised that he had created a taste which he himself knew he could not continue to satisfy. He recognised that opera was developing in a way that was opposed to the principles of his own craft; in particular, he saw that the principles of pure *bel canto* were in decline. In 1806, Samuel Rogers noted in his diary that a soprano had been dissected after death in Bologna, 'to ascertain the power of her voice'. By 1830 this would not have happened. Rossini himself attributed the decline of *bel canto* to the extinction of the castrati, who had in their day been the finest teachers of singing (Isabella Colbran had been taught by one of the very greatest of them, Crescentini). Rossini never ceased to lament the demise of *bel canto*; to the German critic Hanslick in 1860 he said: 'It is at least sixteen years since anyone has known how to sing. They scream, they bellow, they wrestle,' and the main burden of his argument with Wagner that same year was that, in his regretful opinion, Wagner's music would mean the end of pure vocal melody as the basis of musical expression.

But the direction that modern opera was taking which Rossini objected to was only itself a symptom of something more universal, and it was this that Rossini must surely have been responding to when he gave up writing operas. 1830 was not only a year of political crisis in Europe; it was also a watershed in European Romanticism. The first phase of Romanticism had flowered in England and Germany, but by 1830 many of the first generation of Romantics had ceased to be potent creative forces (Wordsworth, Coleridge) or were dead (Keats, Byron, and Shelley). In 1832, Goethe, the most universal writer of the Romantic era, died. But in France and Italy, the countries which affected Rossini, Romanticism did not even properly emerge until the 1820s. The most important literary influence in Italy during Rossini's youth was the neo-classical playwright Alfieri, and his greatest contemporary in the visual arts, Canova, was also a confirmed neo-classicist. The most significant event in the development of Italian Romanticism was the founding of the Milanese journal *Il Conciliatore* in 1818/19, by which time Rossini had written almost thirty operas. The greatest work of Italian Romanticism, Manzoni's *I promessi sposi*, a massive historical novel drawn from the example of Scott, first came out in 1827; by then Rossini was in France, and two years away from his renunciation of opera.

In France itself the picture is much the same. Victor Hugo, considered by most people to be the greatest and most representative figure in French Romanticism, was not born until 1802; his first book of poetry, *Odes*, was published in 1822, the same year as Alfred de Vigny's *Poèmes*; two years previously Lamartine's *Méditations* had appeared. Rossini was more directly affected by drama than poetry, and French theatre, still dominated by the neo-classical ideals of the seventeenth-century playwrights Corneille and Racine, was even slower to give way to Romanticism. Talma, the neo-classical actor who dominated the French stage, only died in 1826. In 1827 the English troupe that introduced Shakespeare to the French arrived in Paris (with such shattering consequences for the twenty-four year old Berlioz and his development as an artist), and it was in that year that Hugo's inflammatory 'Preface' to *Cromwell*, the rallying point for French literary Romanticism, appeared. 1828 saw the publication of Gérard de Nerval's translation of Goethe's *Faust* (which was probably the inspiration for Rossini's plan to base an opera on the work), and 1830 saw Hugo's theories put into practice in his play *Hernani*, whose performance prompted a pitched battle between Classicists and Romantics.

From this brief summary it can be seen that Rossini's career almost entirely predated the emergence of literary Romanticism in Italy and France. If one turns to the expression of Romanticism in

The Battle of Hernani. A painting by Besnard of the famous scene at the Comédie Française when Victor Hugo's Hernani was first performed there in 1830.

music we find that 1830 is an equally important year. In 1826 Weber, one of the few significant composers of the early phase of Romanticism, died, followed in 1827 by Beethoven and in 1828 by Schubert. In 1830, Berlioz' *Symphonie fantastique* was given its first, private performance and in 1831, the year of *Robert le diable*, the twenty-one year old Chopin arrived in Paris. Mendelssohn and Schumann, the most important German romantic composers, were both born within a year of Chopin and of each other.

Several of Rossini's operas reflect an incipient taste for proto-romantic subjects. One of the characteristics of Romanticism is an increased historical consciousness, and *Elisabetta* is an early example of what was to become a passion for plots derived from English history (although by no means the earliest; Mayr had written an opera based on the Wars of the Roses). In *Otello* we have a demonstration of the romantic interest in Shakespeare as an alternative to the neo-classical drama (and poetry) which had for so long dominated the European theatre; and in *La donna del lago*, the first of many European operas based on Scott, with a setting, Scotland, that since Ossian and Scott, was considered more 'romantic' than anywhere. Even an opera like *Semiramide*, with a libretto taken from Voltaire, and which might well be an eighteenth-century *opera seria*, reflects an aspect of Romanticism that drew its inspiration from the exoticism and colour of the east; Delacroix, many of whose paintings demonstrate this particular vein of Romanticism, called *Semiramide* 'truly romantic'.

But although some of Rossini's operas reflect what may be called 'proto-romantic' ideas, ideas that one might say were in the air if not actually articulated, it is fair to say that, unlike Weber, Rossini in these operas never attempted to explore a truly romantic musical language. Rossini was one of a large number of writers, painters and composers who used subject matter that might be considered to have romantic affinities, and indeed might be classified 'Romantic' without developing a comparable means of expression, capable of transforming the basic material.

This is not to deny that Rossini contributed enormously to what eventually became Italian romantic opera, in choice of subject matter and in musical expression, but simply to suggest that by 1830 Rossini was out of tune with the latest developments in Romanticism, and in particular, one aspect of this phase of Romanticism. It is no coincidence that the political events of 1830 happened at the same time as a new wave of Romanticism, for Romanticism was closely allied to political liberalism, if not often to more overtly revolutionary sentiments. It was at this date the phrase 'Romanticism is liberalism in literature' was coined, and in Paris most of the Romantics were metaphorically, if not in person, manning the barricades against the government of Charles X. In Italy, the Romantics suffered more overt persecution for their artistic creed—the 1820 revolt in Naples led to a clampdown throughout Italy, and in Milan two of the most important figures in early Italian Romanticism suffered: Giovanni Berchet, author

Greece on the Ruins of Missalonghi. Delacroix 1826. The figure of Greece appeals for help.

of *La lettera semiseria*, fled Milan, and Silvio Pellico, author of the earliest Italian romantic dramas, was imprisoned by the Austrians in the notorious Spielburg fortress. The Romantics were dangerous to the Austrians because Romanticism was allied to Nationalism. In one sense, Nationalism is simply the concept of romantic individualism writ large; but in Italy it was also part of the attempt to discover an ideal that would transcend state frontiers whilst at the same time remaining specifically Italian; an ideal that might unite the Italian people in sentiment as a prologue to uniting them in political reality. Mazzini, the ideological father of the Risorgimento, understood this perfectly when he wrote of Byron's death: 'I know no more beautiful symbol of the future destiny and mission of art than the death of Byron in Greece. The holy alliance of poetry with the cause of the peoples . . .' The struggle for Greek independence was one of the touchstones of romantic faith. It inspired two of Delacroix' greatest paintings, and in 1824 Beethoven and the Austrian playwright Grillparzer discussed the possibility of an opera based on the subject.

One of Rossini's operas, *Le Siège de Corinthe*, appears to carry oblique references to the struggle being waged in Greece, and two other of his operas, *Mosè/Moïse* and *Guillaume Tell*, have proto-nationalistic subjects. Writers like Balzac and Heine seized on these operas and claimed them as fully-fledged statements of nationalistic ideals. Balzac's novella *Massimilla Doni*, written in 1839, treats *Mosè* as a complete expression of Italian Nationalism, and is full of resounding phrases that proclaim that: 'Moses is the liberator of a nation in slavery', leaving little doubt as to the implications for a present-day nation in slavery. Heine went even further, claiming that Rossinian *opera buffa* too was a focus for nationalistic ideals; he wrote:

Speech is forbidden to the poor Italian slave, so it is through music alone that he can give expression to the emotions of his heart. All his hatred of foreign domination, his longing for freedom, his rage at his impotence, his sorrow on remembering his former lordly greatness, all this is embodied in those melodies. This is the esoteric meaning of *opera buffa*.

But Heine and Balzac were writing after the event. The subject matter of *Le Siège de Corinthe* may have seemed appropriate at a time when Greece was fighting for independence, but we should remember that like *Moïse*, it had originally been conceived well before the Greek struggle had begun. Furthermore, there is nothing to suggest that Rossini was anything but extremely naïve politically, or that in *Le Siège de Corinthe* he was doing more than taking advantage of a respectably fashionable topic.

The case of *Guillaume Tell* is more difficult, for it is a far more overtly romantic and nationalistic opera; its Alpine setting is clearly romantic, and it is full of 'Volkisch' local colour. Above all, it is stirringly and not even obliquely nationalistic, for it treats quite openly the expulsion of the Austrians from an occupied country through the inspiration of a local hero able to unite disparate peoples. And there can be no doubt of its original creator's sentiments, for Schiller was unashamedly liberal and nationalistic. The Austrians themselves were in no doubt as to the danger of the work, and they usually demanded when it was performed in Austrian territory that the characters and setting be altered so that it took place in Scotland; William Tell became William Wallace, and the Austrians became the oppressing English. When performed in Rome it was called *Rudolfo di Stirling*.

Rossini himself called *Guillaume Tell* an opera 'of melancholy tint, peasants, mountains, miseries'. It is a comment which suggests that he disliked some of its more obviously romantic characteristics. A further clue is given in a reply Rossini made to an impresario who wrote to him some time after his retirement from opera asking his permission to stage *Elisabetta* in Florence. Rossini replied: 'These are operas to be left to rest. Give modern music to the public, which loves novelty.' This reply lies at the heart of Rossini's abdication. For all that *Guillaume Tell* possesses most of the qualities which allow us to call it a romantic opera, it is clear that Rossini himself felt uncomfortable with the direction that Romanticism, and as a result romantic opera, was following. He was out of tune with its sensationalism, with its self-obsession, with its lack of propriety, and with its political aspirations. He lamented that 'idealism and sentiment have been exclusively directed in these days to *steam*, to *rapine*, and *barricades*,' and he deplored the setting of librettos that 'magnify unworthy subjects, even horrible crimes' (perhaps a reference to the operas of Donizetti and Verdi). Rossini was not alone in his misgivings. In 1834, his old colleague Jacopo Ferretti prophesied the future of opera:

And since the funeral-pyre, the dagger, and the corrosive sublimate are methods already over-used, and there remains only water and the rope, the last cabaletta will be sung by someone who gurgles it from the depths of a whirlpool and gasps it through the knot of a halter. And in two years time the seven mortal sins will become suitable melodrama all at once, and in four years time even those against nature. The concerted pieces and arie will follow each other without interruption, and recitative will be totally banished.

The prediction was intended to be satirical, but in fact it charts the exact course of opera over the next fifty years. It was a course that Rossini could not follow.

12

Ill health and disappointment

On their way back to Bologna after *Guillaume Tell*, Rossini and Isabella stopped off in Milan, where Rossini met the young Vincenzo Bellini, whose opera *Il pirata* was being performed. Bellini's comments on the meeting show that Rossini already recognised a new spirit in Bellini's music, indication of a more romantic sensibility than his own. He and Isabella then arrived in Bologna in September, where Rossini immediately entered into the operatic life of the city, supervising Giuditta Pasta's début at the Teatro Communale.

As we have seen, Rossini had not yet given up the idea of writing a new opera, although Edouard Robert complained that he was so gregarious that it was difficult to get him to talk seriously about the project. And then in July came the Paris revolution. Rossini took advantage of the change of management at the Opéra to slip free of his obligation to write any further operas for the institution; but when the new government tried to stop his annuity, he was having none of it, and came back to Paris in December 1830 to fight his claim. It was intended as a short visit, and so Isabella was left behind with old 'Vivazza'. Neither, it seems, was very congenial company to the other, and Giuseppe wrote endlessly to Rossini complaining about Isabella's ruinous passion for gambling.

Meanwhile, Rossini had entered into litigation over his claim; it kept him in Paris for five years. It was during these years that the first symptoms of the illness that was to cause him such suffering appeared. In February 1831 he was only just well enough to travel with his friend Aguado to Spain, where in Madrid, after submitting to the usual royal formalities, he made a setting of the famous mediaeval devotional poem the *Stabat Mater* for a Spanish bishop. But he was too ill to attend the première of *Robert le diable* in Paris in November. In May 1832 Aguado took Rossini off for a recuperative visit to Bayonne and Aix-les-Bains, where they stayed until September. In Aix Rossini met Olympe Pelissier. She was a well-known courtesan, whose lovers were said to have included Balzac, the novelist Eugène Sue, and the painter Horace Vernet, for whom she posed as a model. Olympe was thirty-five when Rossini met her, and she became his mistress, nurse-maid, and eventually his wife. When Rossini returned to Paris in September, she took up residence with him.

Although Rossini held no official post in Parisian operatic life, he continued to take an active interest in everything that went on, especially at the Théâtre-Italien, where he acted as unofficial adviser to the directors Severini and Robert. This was the great

Vincenzo Bellini (1801–1835). Heine described Bellini, who was famous for his elegant good looks, as 'a sigh in dancing pumps'. Rossini gave Bellini advice on his score for *I Puritani*.

Grisi, Rubini and Ivanov in Rossini's *Le Siège de Corinthe*. A drawing of 1834 by Queen (then Princess) Victoria, who was a passionate supporter of the Italian opera in London. Giulia Grisi and Giovanni Battista Rubini were members of the famous Puritani quartet. The Russian tenor Nicolai Ivanov was to become a protégé of Rossini's.

age of the Théâtre-Italien, epitomised for most people by the singers who constituted the so-called Puritani quartet, Giulia Grisi, Rubini, Tamburini and Lablache. The other sensation of the time was the daughter of Manuel Garcia, 'the most marvellous of them all, the genius-gifted Malibran' (Rossini's description). Rossini was devoted to Maria Malibran, and later said of her, after her sadly premature death in 1836 aged only twenty-eight that 'she surpassed all her imitators by her disconcerting musical genius, all the women I have ever known by the superiority of her intelligence, the variety of her knowledge and her flashing temperament'. In 1831 Chopin wrote home that he had heard Malibran singing the role of Otello in Rossini's opera, and in 1832 Rossini wrote a piece specially for her, the cantata *Giovanna d'Arco* ('Joan of Arc'), which he dedicated to Olympe Pelissier.

The superb collection of singers at the Théâtre-Italien attracted many composers, in particular Bellini, whom Rossini lured to Paris in August 1833. Once in Paris, Bellini stayed, writing that he did so because of the quality of the singers at the Théâtre-Italien. Bellini courted Rossini assiduously, and described him as the 'musical oracle of Paris'; in January 1835 Bellini's *I Puritani* especially written for Paris, was produced, and Rossini followed the rehearsals for the new work closely, at Bellini's request. But

121

Maria Malibran (1808–1836) as Desdemona in *Otello* (she also sang the role of Otello itself). The daughter of Manuel Garcia, Rossini's first Almaviva. Painting by Henri Decaisne.

Rossini was also intent on securing Donizetti for Paris, and in March 1835 Donizetti's *Marino Faliero* was performed at the Théâtre-Italien, much to the dismay of the neurotically touchy Bellini, who imagined, ungratefully, that he was being replaced in Rossini's favours by Donizetti. In September, Bellini died, at the age of only thirty-four. Rossini was one of the pallbearers at the funeral, and made many of the necessary arrangements for the occasion, a mark of his devotion to the younger composer.

In 1834 Rossini made a brief trip back to Bologna, but the fight over his annuity was not resolved, in his favour, until 1835. That year he visited Belgium, where he travelled for the first and last time on a train, and Germany, where he met the young Mendelssohn in Frankfurt, and then in October returned to Bologna. Olympe had to be left behind, but in February 1837, Rossini began the proceedings of separation from Isabella, which were completed by September. Meanwhile, in March, Olympe had arrived from Paris, and in November, so that they could live together, the situation in Bologna having become too uncomfortable, Rossini and Olympe moved to Milan.

1838 was the year of the Coronation in Milan of the Emperor Ferdinand as King of Lombardy. Liszt who was in Milan at this same date with his mistress Marie d'Agoult (who, in a reprehensible display of hypocrisy refused to receive Olympe) described the surprisingly warm reception that the Emperor received from the Milanese, and an Austrian, Alexander Hübner, wrote:

It was a time of reconciliation. The salon of Prince Metternich was the gathering place for the Lombardy aristocracy. Beside Pasta, with Rossini at the piano, we heard Prince Belgiojoso sing, just returned home from exile.

Liszt described Rossini's musical activities further:

Rossini, become rich, idle, and illustrious, has opened his home to his compatriots, and during the entire winter a numerous society has filled his salon . . . There are few cities in Europe in which music is cultivated as much as it is in Milan.

Rossini's contentment was short-lived, for a series of sorrows struck. In January 1838 the Théâtre-Italien was burned down; Rossini's friend Severini was killed trying to escape, and Robert, his associate, was seriously injured. Then Rossini's own illness struck again. The form it took—urethritis and related afflictions—suggests that some form of venereal disease was the trouble. He returned to Bologna in March, partly because of the increasing frailty of his father, who in April 1839 died, aged eighty. That same year his friend the French tenor Nourrit, depressed at what he thought was the premature failure of his career, killed himself in Naples. Rossini himself went to Naples to stay with Barbaja at his villa at Posilippo in an attempt to recover from the series of shocks.

Despite all this, Rossini had not given up his interest in musical life. He had taken up a new protégé, the Russian tenor Ivanov, and in January 1839 he had been approached by the Liceo in Bologna and asked to take up a position as official advisor, and effectively, unofficial director. He accepted in April, but was not able to perform his first duties until January 1840. He established weekly concerts there, and wrote to Domenico Donzelli in Vienna requesting him to send music by Weber and Mendelssohn to be performed at these concerts, showing that he was still trying to keep abreast of developments in German music.

In 1841, a curious set of circumstances led to the completion of one of the two major works that Rossini wrote after 1830, the *Stabat Mater*. It had been written, it will be recalled, for a Spanish bishop, but on the condition that it should remain privately in the bishop's hands. In 1837, however, the bishop died, and his executors sold the score to the publisher Aulagnier, who wrote to Rossini telling him that he intended to publish. Rossini then revealed that he had not completed the work himself, and set about finishing it so that his own publisher Troupenas had a rival, and authentic, edition to produce. The newly completed work was given its first performance in Paris in January 1842, at the Théâtre-Italien, with Grisi, Mario (the latest sensation amongst Italian tenors) and Tamburini singing. It is a work full of both strength and charm, written largely in an unapologetically operatic style, and quite free of the lachrymose piety that the text could so easily have prompted in any composer but Rossini. It shows that Rossini had no need of the extra two years of counterpoint lessons that Padre Mattei expected of him, and in several sections attains a degree of drama that would not have been unworthy of Verdi's *Requiem*. Rossini, like Verdi, could not help writing dramatic music, even to a sacred text.

The *Stabat Mater* was first heard by Rossini in Bologna in March 1842, when Donizetti, whom Rossini admired and trusted, was asked to conduct three performances. Rossini was also hoping that he might be able to entice Donizetti to take up the post of Professor of harmony and counterpoint at the Liceo. Unfortunately, his pleadings arrived at the same moment as an invitation to Vienna, which Donizetti accepted instead. Meanwhile, the performance of the *Stabat Mater* had brought back to Rossini all the trappings of his years of success; he was given a banquet, and the town band played the usual selections of his music. On his name-day that same year a civic reception was mounted, with fireworks and a magnificent hot-air balloon. The city could not let it be thought that the genius in its midst had been forgotten, and the celebrations became an annual event.

They could not keep Rossini in Bologna, though, for his continued ill-health led him to cast around for cures, and finally sent him back to Paris, where the famous surgeon Jean Civiale had made a special study of treatments for gallstones, from which Rossini appeared to be suffering. So in May 1843, Rossini set off for Paris. The previous year, Aguado, possibly his greatest friend, had died in a mountain storm on his way to Spain, and when Rossini and Olympe got caught in a fearsome storm on the Mont Cenis pass, he must have recalled the sad fate of his friend with some apprehension.

The stay in Paris was short—only four months, three of which were spent in virtual isolation—but during this time some 2,000 people were said to have called on Rossini. In September, content that Doctor Civiale's cure had worked, he returned to Bologna, where one of the first events he attended was a performance of Verdi's third opera *Nabucco*. He must have liked what he heard, for he subsequently asked Verdi to write an aria for his protégé the Russian tenor Ivanov, and he always took a keen, if wary interest in the development of Verdi's career.

In October 1845, his wife Isabella died at her villa at Castenaso.

The scene of rejoicing at the election of Pius IX in 1846. The Roman crowd pulls the Pope's carriage through the streets.

It was a sad ending, lonely and forgotten, for the great *prima donna*, and Rossini was genuinely upset. But it freed him to wed Olympe, who had by now proved herself to be a devoted and loving companion and nurse, and they were married after a decent interval of ten months. The more sophisticated of the visitors to the Rossini household seem to have found Olympe coarse and ignorant, but there can be no doubt that, with her essentially simple ways she was the ideal wife for Rossini whose increasing ill health meant that he now needed constant attention. Olympe was as solicitous of her husband's reputation as of his health, and was fiercely loyal to him until her death ten years after his own.

In 1846 the reactionary Pope Gregory XVI died. His successor was Cardinal Mastai Ferretti, born the same year as Rossini, who took the name Pius IX, more familiar in its Italian form Pio Nono. The new Pope had a reputation as a liberal, and people responded quickly to any hope of change. Mazzini and Garibaldi, the freedom fighters of the Risorgimento, both wrote to the new Pope, and from Bologna came a petition to the new ruler of the Papal States for governmental reform; it was drawn up by a prominent local politician, Mario Minghetti, and one of the signatories was Rossini. He also adapted a chorus from *La donna del lago* for the

Pope, and wrote a cantata 'of gratitude and praise'. Pius did not disappoint his supporters, and instituted a series of cautious reforms, long overdue, throughout his states.

But the events of 1848 soon put an end to reform. 1848, like 1830, was a year of revolution throughout Europe. In February, King Louis-Philippe of France was overthrown in Paris, and a short-lived Republic established. In March, Metternich was finally toppled from power in Vienna. In Italy there was a rising in Palermo in January, and the resultant granting of a democratic constitution in the Kingdom of the Two Sicilies was followed by similar concessions in Piedmont, Tuscany, and Rome. A revolution in Milan in March succeeded in expelling the Austrians, and in Venice a Republic was established under Daniele Manin. The Austrians fought to keep their dominions, and the other states of northern Italy, Tuscany, Lombardy, Lucca, Parma, and Modena, rallied in defence of the new independence offered under the banner of the Kingdom of Piedmont. The Pope decreed against his own states joining to support the rebels, but his decree was largely ineffective, and troops and funds were raised in Bologna amongst other places. Rossini, who was quite prepared to append his name to a document for reform, did not show any marked enthusiasm for the more overtly revolutionary spirit of some of his fellow Bolognese, and in April he was shouted at and booed by a band of volunteers on their way to fight for the new cause. Rossini was so alarmed by the hostility shown him, and by the violence in the streets of Bologna, that he and Olympe fled across the Apennines to the safety of Florence.

News of what had happened to the local celebrity filtered back to Bologna, and Rossini's patriotism was quickly defended; the patriot and priest Father Ugo Bassi, one of Garibaldi's closest followers, publicly asserted Rossini's love for his fatherland in the Basilica of San Petronio in Bologna. Rossini was begged to return, but pleaded his wife's indisposition, though he did agree to set a patriotic text by Bassi to music. In the event Bassi was wounded in a battle, and Rossini set a text by another author.

In August 1848 Charles Albert, King of Piedmont, finally capitulated to the Austrians. The following year the Republic that Mazzini had managed to establish in Rome was overthrown, and the defenders, led by Garibaldi, fled north. Amongst them was Ugo Bassi, who was captured and shot by the Austrians. Only Venice now held out against the Austrian domination of Italy, and by the end of the year Venice too had fallen.

In September 1849 Rossini considered it safe to return to Bologna to sort out his neglected affairs. The Austrians were everywhere, and Rossini, naïve enough not to recognise the hostility shown towards them by the Bolognese, allowed himself to be seen in the company of Austrians. The ill-will that this aroused in his fellow citizens, and the tension in the city, forced him back to Florence in May 1851, embittered and sad. He was never again to return to the city he considered his home.

The years between 1851 and 1855 were spent in Florence. Florençe was by now a popular and fashionable visiting place for English travellers, and among the well-known English people living there at this date were Fanny Trollope, mother of Anthony Trollope and a writer in her own right, and the newly married Elizabeth and Robert Browning. But Rossini was too ill to concern himself with society. He reported that he was suffering from hydrophobia, probably due to the tormenting pain caused by a permanent infection of the urinary system, and he showed all the symptoms of what was then called extreme neurasthenia. Visits were paid to Montecatini Terme, today rather a drab little spa that lies in the Arno valley between Florence and Pisa, and to Bagni di Lucca, a more attractive spa lying in the mountains north of Lucca, much beloved of Shelley. But he got no better; he could not be persuaded to take an interest in anything, and those who knew him feared for his sanity and his life. Finally it was decided that only a return to Paris and the most advanced medical care could save him, and so in April 1855, he and Olympe set off for the last time on the journey across Europe to Paris. Rossini, remembering his experience of 1835, still refused to travel by train, and the journey took over a month.

13

The last years

The Paris Rossini returned to in 1855 was very different from that he had left in 1843. The Republic which had been set up after the overthrow of Louis-Philippe had given way, after a *coup d'état*, to the renewed Imperial ambitions of the Bonaparte dynasty, and Napoleon's nephew Louis-Napoleon was now, as Napoleon III, ruler of France.

The news of Rossini's arrival in Paris coincided with the news from the Crimea, where France and England, allies at last, were fighting Russia. But the Parisians seemed almost more excited by Rossini's return; people flocked to see him, but apart from a few favoured friends such as Auber, Carafa, Lionel de Rothschild (Rossini's host on the trip to Belgium and Germany in 1835), the crowds were turned away, for Rossini was still far too frail to receive visitors. By June he was well enough to see Verdi, who was in Paris for the opening of his opera *Les Vêpres siciliennes*, and in July he went to Trouville, the resort on the Norman coast much favoured by the Empress Eugénie. It was on this trip that he met the German composer Ferdinand Hiller, friend of Schumann and conductor of the Théâtre-Italien in 1852 and 1853, who kept a record of their conversations that is one of the most valuable sources for Rossini's own views on his life and career. The visit did Rossini's health some good, and the following year he felt strong enough to venture further afield to the German spa towns of Wildblad and Kissingen, where he was presented to King Maximilian II of Bavaria, the father of Wagner's patron Ludwig II.

Increasingly good health allowed him to indulge in his normal gregariousness (and no doubt increased contact with society improved his health further). Rossini himself did not dine out, except very occasionally with his closest friends; but his apartment on the corner of the Chaussée d'Antan and the Boulevard des Italiens, on a site next to the house in which Mozart stayed in Paris, became one of the most active centres of Parisian musical society. To start with, Rossini held small dinners on Saturday evenings which were followed by a little musical entertainment, but these soon turned into the famous 'Samedi Soirs', the first of which was held in 1858, and at various times over the next ten years the greatest musicians in Paris came to perform at them. Among the most regular attenders were Rossini's old friends and would-be rivals Auber and Meyerbeer, but at any given moment the visitor might expect to find there, amongst others, Verdi (for whom the quartet from *Rigoletto* was specially performed) and the

Rossini's apartment in the appropriately named Boulevard des Italiens.

young Boito; the pianists Anton Rubinstein, Thalberg, and Liszt, who played his *Légendes* at a 'Samedi Soir' concert; the French composers Gounod, Ambroise Thomas, and Bizet, who was introduced to Rossini after jointly winning a competition for a one-act operetta set up by Offenbach, and who became a regular attender. The greatest French baritone of the time, Jean-Baptiste Fauré, was a frequent performer, and one evening Maria Taglioni, the legendary dancer of the romantic era who had danced in the première of *Guillaume Tell* and was now living in retirement, came and danced a minuet and gavotte. The most frequently performed composer at these concerts was Mozart, but Rossini's own latest compositions were sometimes introduced, a task which Rossini entrusted to Saint-Saëns.

Rossini had not given up composing altogether. Ever since his retirement from opera he had continued to write small pieces, many of them songs, and even more for piano solo. A collection of his vocal pieces had been published in 1835 under the title *Soirées Musicales*, and both Liszt and Wagner had made arrangements of numbers from it. Now back in Paris, Rossini set about composing

A lithograph showing Rossini composing at the piano.

again. He called the pieces he wrote his *Péchés de vieillesse*, or 'Sins of old-age', and gave them witty titles that indicate he did not intend them to be taken too seriously. Volume IV of these collected pieces is entitled: 'Four hors d'oeuvres and four beggars for the piano', and the pieces themselves are as follows: Radishes, Anchovies, Gherkins, Butter; and Dried Figs ('There we are—Bonjour Madame'), Almonds ('Midnight sounds—Bonsoir, Madame'), Hazelnuts ('To my dear Nini—a message of love to my dog') and Grapes ('To my little parakeet—dammit, dammit'). Bonjour, Rossini! Bonjour, farceur!—Oh, m'head—Oh, m'head—To attention—Ready—take aim—fire! rataplan, rataplan, rataplan [a dig at Meyerbeer's *Les Huguenots*]. When I drink red wine, everything turns in the inn.' Other titles include *A Nightmare, Impromptu anodine, Prelude convulsif* and *Un petit Train de plaisir*, to which is appended a gruesome description of a terrible derailment and the death of two passengers, recalling Rossini's aversion to railway travel.

Rossini's *Péchés de vieillesse* are inclined to outstay their welcome, often over-using some harmonic trick so that it becomes wearisome; but many of them have a melodic charm curiously reminiscent of Chopin, which reminds us of Chopin's admiration for Bellini's music, and the closeness of Chopin's florid melodies to the Italian *bel canto* style.

Rossini very rarely attended musical occasions in Paris outside

130

his own home, making rare exceptions only when music by one of his close friends was being performed. Nonetheless, he continued to take a keen interest in everything that went on; the German critic Hanslick, who visited him in 1860, described Rossini as, 'a disinterested spectator who watches without any envy or bitterness, though not always without irony'. One of the *Péchés* is a parody of Offenbach, which shows Rossini's awareness of the most fashionable developments in music at the time. His own operas continued to be performed: by the 1850s the Théâtre-Italien was in bad straits, severely challenged by the ascendancy and popularity of French opera, but in 1855 there had been a full revival of *Mosè*, and in 1856 of *La Cenerentola*. In 1859, news reached Paris that two sisters, Barbara and Carlotta Marchisio, had sung in a triumphant revival of *Semiramide* at La Scala. Their success was such that they were engaged to sing in the same opera at the Opéra in Paris. The musical preparation was entrusted to Rossini's old friend and colleague Carafa, the man whom Berlioz described bitterly as, 'a nonentity, a musical odd-job man whose

Rossini being applauded by the audience at a performance of one of his works at the Opéra.

only recommendation is that he is not French'. Rossini went to hear a rehearsal and was ecstatic, believing that he had at last heard true *bel canto* again.

The most remarkable of the visits that Rossini received during the last years in Paris was that of Richard Wagner, who went to see the old composer in March 1860 when he was in Paris conducting a series of concerts of his music, including the Prelude to his recently completed (although still unperformed) *Tristan und Isolde*, and arranging for *Tannhäuser* to be performed at the Opéra the following year. Both Wagner and Rossini were wary of each other: Wagner of Rossini because there were many witticisms at his expense circulating round Paris ascribed to Rossini, witticisms which were, as Michotte put it, 'of a taste as dubious as they were apocryphal;' and Rossini of Wagner because he was aware that Wagner had written dismissively of his music (there is a cruel attack on the *Stabat Mater* in *Oper und Drama*) and was probably aware that Wagner was inclined to be equally dismissive of the man.

The meeting was arranged and recorded by Edmond Michotte, a friend of Rossini and a member of Wagner's circle in Paris. Wagner, who was anyway sensitive about his reputation in Paris, agreed on the meeting with some trepidation although much curiosity—could Rossini really be the degenerate bon-viveur and gourmet portrayed in the popular imagination? In the event, the meeting was as touching as that between Rossini and Beethoven many years previously. Rossini's tone was throughout a model of tactful restraint, especially since Wagner was inclined to get carried away in his denunciations of the old school of operatic practice, forgetting that he was in the presence of its greatest practitioner. Rossini listened with good-humoured tolerance, occasionally answering with a little gentle, smiling irony. He agreed with Wagner's condemnation of some of the more absurd excesses of his native school, and with a shrug admitted his own subservience to convention. When Wagner launched into praise of *Guillaume Tell*, Rossini's comment (and one can see the twinkle in his eye, although Wagner wouldn't have done) was: 'So I made music of the future without knowing it?' to which Wagner earnestly added: 'There, maestro, you made music for all times, and that is the best.'

The conversation turned to Weber and Beethoven, and to Rossini's own musical education and career. Rossini was able to demonstrate what to Wagner was a surprising understanding of German music, saying of Bach, 'he is an overwhelming genius. If Beethoven is a prodigy of humanity, Bach is a miracle'. By the end of the meeting Wagner's view of Rossini as a man had changed a good deal. 'Rossini,' he said, 'is caricatured as a great epicurean, stuffed not with music—of which he was emptied long ago—but with mortadella.' After the meeting, he described Rossini as 'simple, natural, serious'.

Rossini seems to have been in good health again and able to

enjoy his final years. He had always had a tendency to stoutness, and was now undeniably corpulent. Nonetheless, this did not stop him from taking regular strolls along the Champs-Elysées, often walking the whole length from the Place de la Concorde to the Place d l'Etoile, and he was a familiar figure on the boulevards, respectfully pointed out by passers-by. It was during these last years in Paris that his reputation as a gourmet and *bon-viveur* grew up, and certainly, free of the pressures of composition and the restrictions of ill health, he allowed himself to indulge the pleasures of life to the full. In 1859 he started to build a villa for himself in the fashionable suburb of Passy, and from 1861 onwards the Rossinis would move there every spring, and stay throughout the summer. It was in Passy that Hanslick met Rossini, and described 'the sparkle of his brown eyes, intelligent and friendly', and the 'rather long though beautifully shaped nose, the fine, sensuous mouth, and the round chin which testified to the old Italian's former good looks'. Rossini had gone bald young, and in his middle age took to wearing wigs, described by one visitor as being 'the most wiggy of wigs'; when it was cold, he would pile several wigs on his head at once.

In the 1860s Rossini found himself writing public music again, almost invariably at the request of friends. In 1862 he was asked to supply something for the Great Exhibition in London and declined, but when Auber, the director of the Paris Conservatoire, asked him for a piece for a fund-raising event for a monument to Cherubini (who had died in 1842), Rossini obliged by arranging a vocal cantata which he had previously written for a private performance called *Le Chant des Titans* ('The Song of the Titans') which was performed at the Opéra in December 1861. In 1863 he wrote an even larger work, the *Petite Messe Solonnelle*, a setting of the Mass for four soloists, choir, and accompaniment of harmonium and two pianos. Rossini prefaced the *Petite Messe* with a dedication to God: 'I was born for *opera buffa* as well Thou knowest. Little skill, a little heart, and that is all. So be Thou blessed, and admit me to paradise.'

The first performance of the *Petite Messe* was a private one at the home of his friend the Comte Pillet-Will, in March 1864. It was the occasion of one of the last meetings between Rossini and Meyerbeer, who was already mortally ill, and who died two months later. In 1867, probably because of a request from his former pupil and regular correspondent Michael Costa, now an important figure in English musical life, Rossini set a text for the Birmingham Festival. The same year he was chairman of a committee set up to award a prize for the best composition submitted for the Paris International Exhibition of 1867. The prize was awarded to Saint-Saëns, but much to that composer's chagrin, Rossini himself decided to write a piece, and presented it to the Emperor. It was entitled:

To Napoleon III and his valiant People. Hymn (with accompaniment for

The Exposition Universelle of 1867. A painting by Edouard Manet.

Grand Orchestra and Military Band) for Baritone (solo), a Pontiff. Chorus of High Priests, Chorus of Vivandieres, Soldiers and People. Dances, Bells, Drums, and Canons. Forgive such meagreness!

The *Hymn* was performed with an orchestra of 800 players.

In 1868 the Opéra celebrated the 500th performance of *Guillaume Tell*, and Rossini was serenaded with selections from the opera performed by the entire orchestra and chorus of the Opéra; a noisy serenade. He was now rising seventy-six, and his health was failing. But that year he received a letter from the Minister of Education in Italy in which the Minister lamented the decline of music in Italy since Rossini had ceased composing, and invited him to become the President of a society to be called the Società Rossiniana, dedicated to the reform of Italian music. Not surprisingly, when news of the scheme reached the ears of people like Verdi, they were insulted and indignant, and some of their anger fell on Rossini himself. Rossini hastened to retract his support, and with the fall of the Italian government, the scheme came to nothing. But it showed Rossini still to be taking an active, if misguided, interest in contemporary music.

Probably in 1868, Rossini was given the title Grand Knight of the Order of the Crown of Italy. It was the last of many decorations that Rossini received in his lifetime, stretching back to 1829, when he had been awarded the Légion d'honneur after the première of *Guillaume Tell*. Since then he had received decorations from Germany, Belgium, Spain, Mexico, and of course, Italy. In recognition of the last honour conferred, Rossini composed a piece called *La corona d'Italia*, scored for military band, including parts for the saxophone. His accompanying letter read: 'I cannot imagine that the leaders of the Italian military bands have not adopted these instruments.'

In September 1868, the last of the 'Samedi Soirs' took place. Rossini was too frail to act as host, and in October his condition deteriorated. He was suffering from a lung infection, and then

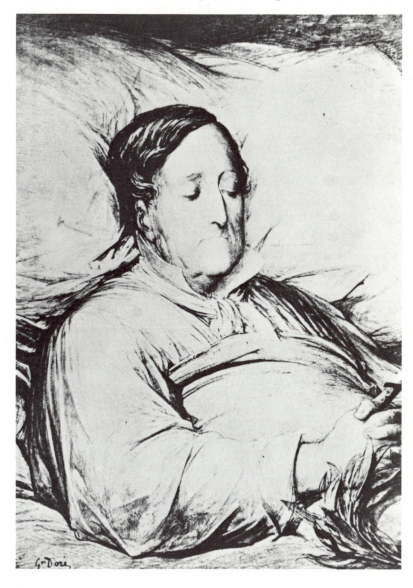

Rossini on his deathbed. An engraving after a drawing by Gustav Doré. The young Doré had been introduced to Rossini only a few months earlier at one of the last Samedi Soirs, and was summoned to draw Rossini as he lay on his death bed.

135

developed what was probably cancer of the rectum. In November he was operated on in the villa at Passy, and after a brief recovery, declined again. It was clear that he was dying, and Olympe, with the piety typical of an ex-courtesan, persuaded him to receive the Last Sacrament. Some of his closest friends gathered to attend as the end drew near, and on Thursday, November 12, in the presence of Adelina Patti, Alboni, and Tamburini, Rossini received extreme unction, and the following day, Friday 13, he died.

The next day the young painter and engraver Gustav Doré came and sketched Rossini on his death bed. The corpse was then embalmed and put in its coffin, and taken to the Church of the Madeleine to await the funeral, which took place in church of La Trinité. Some 4,000 people attended, and the music for the occasion was organised by the eighty-six year old Auber. The coffin was then taken to the Père Lachaise Cemetery, where Rossini was buried alongside the other expatriots Cherubini, Bellini, and Chopin.

Rossini's funeral. From the Illustrated London News.

In Italy, Verdi sprang into action, and only four days after Rossini's death began to plan a *Requiem* to be written in Rossini's memory by thirteen different composers, each of whom would

contribute a section; Verdi himself would write the *Libera me*, which he completed. The whole project was an indication of Verdi's recognition of Rossini's enormous contribution to Italian opera, a contribution that he must have felt some of the lesser contemporaries had forgotten, for the rest of the project came to nothing.

In 1878 Olympe died, respected and respectable, and in 1887 Rossini's body was returned to Italy, not to a city with which he had been closely associated, but to Florence, where it was put in Santa Croce, the church which, since Unification, had become the national Pantheon of Italy. In 1912 a fitting tomb was erected.

Bibliography

The biographer of Rossini soon faces the problem that Rossini's life divides neatly into two halves, and that the earlier, active phase of his life is far less well documented than is the latter phase when he had ceased to compose operas.

The standard work of biography is G. Radiciotti's two volume *Gioacchino Rossini: vita documentata, opere ed influenze su l'arte* (Tivoli. 1927–9). In English the most complete account of Rossini's life is to be found in H. Weinstock *Rossini: A Biography* (New York 1968). More enjoyable, but with few pretensions to scholarship are G. H. Derwent's affectionate *Rossini and some forgotten Nightingales* (London 1934), and Francis Toye *Rossini: a study in Tragicomedy* (London 1934). For a comprehensive account of Rossini's development as a composer readers should consult the entry made under *Rossini* in *The New Grove*, Vol 16 (London 1980) by P. Gossett.

Stendhal's *La Vie de Rossini* (Paris 1824) is a work of polemical journalism, not to say propaganda, and should be read as such. Nonetheless, both this and *Rome, Naples et Florence en 1817* also by Stendhal provide a fascinating picture of the period, and the worst inaccuracies and deliberate misleadings can be checked against Stendhal's *Journals* (1817). The first two have been translated by R. N. Coe.

Of the many contemporary accounts of Rossini later in his life, the most interesting is that which records Wagner's visit to Rossini in 1860 by E. Michotte *Souvenirs personnels: la visite de Richard Wagner à Rossini* (Paris 1906; trans H. Weinstock 1968). Its authenticity has been doubted, since Michotte did not publish until forty years after the event, but its contents in no way contradict the picture we have of Rossini in old age.

Index

WORKS BY ROSSINI

Operas